GW00503720

INDY CAFE COOKBOOK

Publisher: Salt Media

Editor: Kathryn Lewis

Copy editors: Kathryn Lewis, Abi Manning, Jo Rees, Rosanna Rothery

Editorial assistants: Sophie Ellis, Selena Young

Production manager: Kate Fenton

Art direction and design: Christopher Sheppard

Photography: Reece Leung 54; Evie Johnstone 147, p174; Christopher Sheppard 6, 18, 22, 24, 36, 46, 49, 55, 65, 100, 181, 116, 153, 200, 202

www.indycoffee.guide

ISBN 978 1 9996478 2 7

First published in Great Britain in 2018 by Salt Media Ltd

Text © 2018 Salt Media Ltd

Design and layout © 2018 Salt Media Ltd

Printed in Great Britain

salt media

www.saltmedia.co.uk

01271 859299   ideas@saltmedia.co.uk

The right of Salt Media to be identified as the author of this work has been asserted by it in accordance with the Copyright, Designs and Patents Act 1988.

A catalogue record of the book is available from the British Library.

All rights reserved. No part of this publication may be reproduced, distributed, or transmitted in any form or by any means, including photocopying, recording, or other electronic or mechanical methods, without the prior written permission of the publisher, except in the case of brief quotations embodied in critical reviews and certain other non-commercial uses permitted by copyright law.

For permission requests, email Salt Media Ltd.

While every effort has been made to ensure the accuracy of the information in this publication, we cannot be held responsible for any errors or omissions and take no responsibility for the consequences of error or for any loss or damage suffered by users of any of the information published on any of these pages.

MIX
Paper from
responsible sources
FSC® C010353
www.fsc.org

CON-TENTS

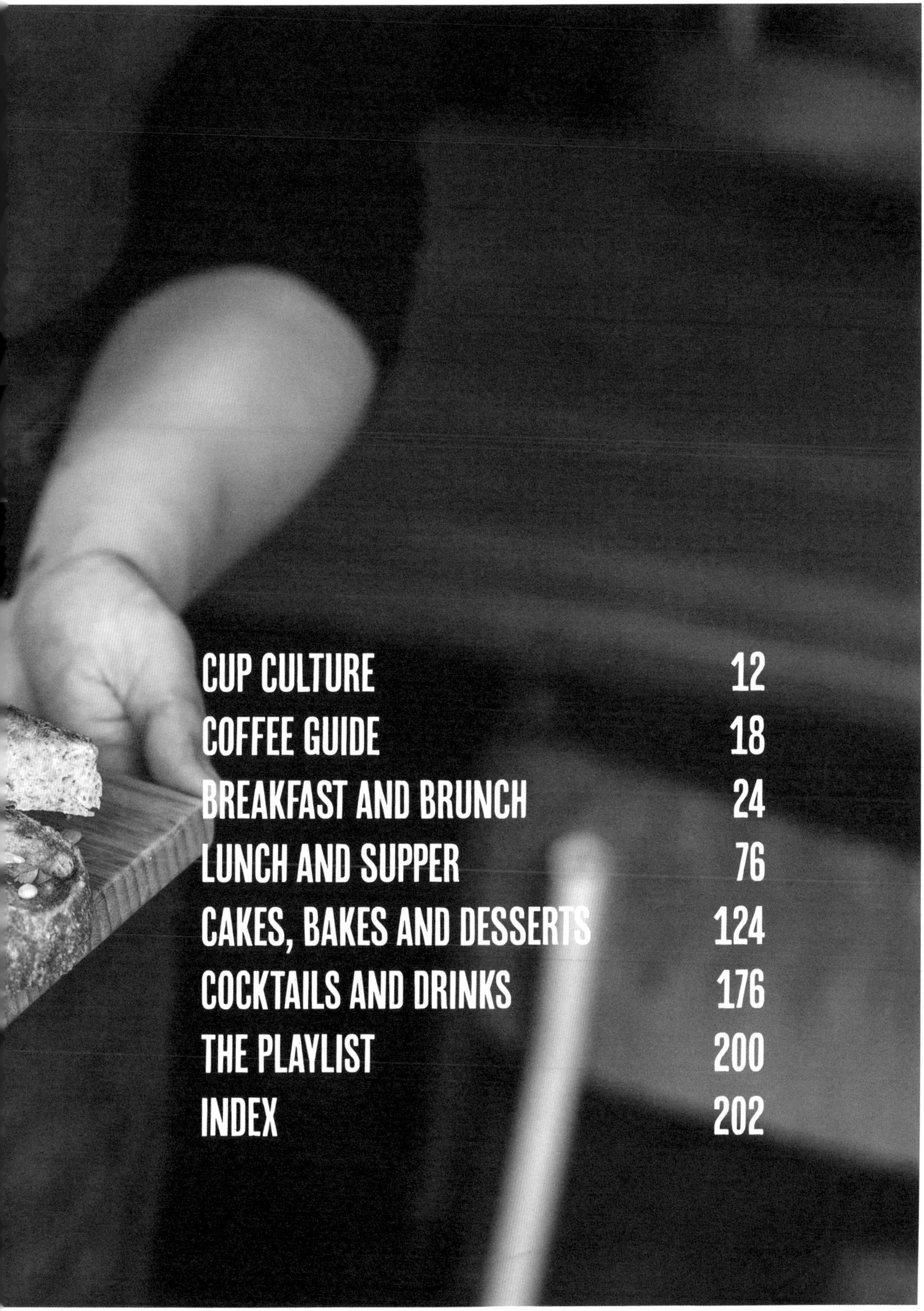

Ever wanted to know how your favourite cafe makes its grilled cheese so gooey, or how to recreate the showstopping carrot cake from your go-to indie coffee shop?

The team behind the *Independent Coffee Guides* have been table hopping across the UK and Ireland to round up the best brunch dishes, colourful lunches, Insta-ready bakes and coffee-infused cocktails in the first speciality coffee shop-inspired cookbook.

The carefully curated selection of signature dishes come hot from the kitchens of 40 of the leading speciality cafes and roasteries in the UK and Ireland.

Each recipe has been matched with a coffee and playlist pairing so you can recreate a slice of cafe culture at home.

Enjoy!

Indy Coffee Guide team

CUP
CULTURE

Speciality coffee is flourishing in the UK and Ireland: we've latched onto the good stuff, ditched the pub in favour of cafe catch-ups, discovered coffee shops as co-working spaces and even squeezed a fourth meal (brunch) into the weekend. We lift the lid on the scene – and take a look at where it's heading

THE COFFEE SCENE

From the shiny-faced *Friends* cast chugging massive cappuccinos at Central Perk to millennials Instagramming photos of their misspelt names on big brand takeaway cups, the last two decades have seen coffee reach beyond the domestic realm to become a social experience.

In the UK and Ireland, global chains such as Costa, Starbucks and Caffé Nero have dominated the ever-growing cafe scene. And with Coca-Cola investing £3.9bn in the purchase of Costa in 2018, the big boys' control of the market shows no sign of abating.

However, alongside the chains' commodity-grade coffee offering, a niche speciality coffee scene has quietly flourished, which is all about independence, quality and authenticity.

The cafes are run by couples, friends and families who are committed to serving high quality, speciality-grade beans from indie roasters – often accompanied by homemade food.

Supporting farmers through sustainable trade – both at home and across the coffee growing regions of the world – is a priority, along with a focus on flavour and exemplary service.

'The number of speciality coffee shops and roasteries in the UK and Ireland has soared in the last five years,' says James Shepherd of the Specialty Coffee Association (SCA). *'People with an interest in good coffee have seen the exciting scene in Australia and New Zealand and want to create a slice of antipodean caffeine culture at home.'*

WHAT THE CUP IS SPECIALITY COFFEE?

Simply put, speciality coffee has been graded as a higher quality product than commodity coffee, which is what you'll drink in the chains – and almost everywhere else.

This coffee is tracked from plant to cup, and sourced from farms which are paid fairly for their crop.

Once purchased, the green beans are lightly roasted in small batches

'If you care where your food comes from and are prepared to pay a small amount more for a high quality product, you probably drink speciality coffee'

to optimise their unique flavour potential. This is a key difference to commodity coffee, which is usually roasted dark and as a result lacks the rainbow of flavours found in speciality.

In order to maintain these carefully developed notes, the beans are freshly ground to order before being expertly prepared by skilled baristas – either as espresso-based drinks (such as flat whites and cappuccino) or via a range of filter brewing methods.

If you're the kind of person who cares where their food comes from, buys local and supports ethical farming and is prepared to pay more for a high quality product, you probably drink speciality coffee.

FLAT WHAT?

Infiltrating the cafe vocabulary of Australia and New Zealand (both nations fiercely defend their claim to the term) in the early noughties, the flat white has been the poster cup for the speciality movement.

Hardcore baristas sweat the small stuff (crafting the perfect cup is all in the detail) but a flat white is usually a 6oz drink made with a double shot of quality espresso, gently steamed whole milk and a thin layer of velvety smooth micro-foam fashioned into a latte art design.

GOOD COFFEE DESERVES GOOD GRUB

Speciality coffee has developed its niche audience over a couple of decades, and now reaches beyond the large cities and even into the wilds (if you look carefully you'll find speciality served in some very remote spots).

Yet indie cafe owners know that flat whites and traybakes alone won't pay the rent. So they've embraced the serving of simple but delicious, freshly-made food to complement the bill of quality drinks.

From breakfast to brunch to afternoon bakes and cakes, you're pretty much guaranteed to eat well (and ethically) at speciality coffee shops. The SCA's James Shepherd thinks that antipodean culture is an influence here, too:

'The brunch market in speciality hotspots such as Melbourne is huge and [UK and Ireland] cafe owners have taken inspiration from their pared-back menus.'

Paying the same attention to the sourcing, sustainability and quality of food as they do to coffee, these speciality cafe owners champion local producers and seasonal ingredients in dishes that are fresh, unprocessed and unpretentious – while often being pretty indulgent, too.

The scene also influences mainstream food culture, largely as a result of its constant reinvention and quick response to new trends such as the growth in plant-based eating. If you're in any doubt, just think how ubiquitous avocado on toast and gourmet doughnuts have become ...

WHAT'S NEXT FOR SPECIALITY?

As independent coffee shops have become more popular (and, in turn, more profitable), developments are afoot.

Cafe owners are launching second (and third) outposts of their original concept, and increasingly exploring the realms of coffee roasting.

'This trend is going to continue,' comments James. 'We're going to see more owners roasting beans to stock their cafes and then we'll see more roasteries owning coffee farms at origin.'

In the same way that some cafe owners are exerting control over the quality of the coffee they serve by roasting it in-house, they're also increasingly producing their own sourdough bread and carby delights alongside the homemade cakes. The sweet result is the burgeoning cafe bakery trend.

Getting creative with preserving, curing and fermenting is also on the up.

'They want to take more of the chain into their own hands – from farm to cup and field to plate,' asserts James.

'Some of the most exciting food in the UK and Ireland at the moment is appearing on all-day brunch menus or being served after dark at cafe supper clubs and pop-up events.'

We'll raise a cup to that.

COFFEE GUIDE
ESPRESSO DRINKS

ESPRESSO DRINKS

Words by **Callum Parsons** of Extract Coffee Roasters

ESPRESSO (1)

A concentrate of coffee created by pushing water through finely ground beans at pressure.

AMERICANO (2)

Espresso diluted with hot water to reduce strength to taste.

FLAT WHITE (3)

Espresso topped with velvety steamed milk. Served in a 6-8oz cup for the best balance of milk to coffee.

CAPPUCCINO (4)

Espresso with a thicker foam giving a fuller mouthfeel. Served in a 6-8oz cup with an optional dusting of cocoa.

CORTADO (5)

An equal measure of espresso to steamed milk 1:1. Served in a 4oz cup.

PICCOLO

Espresso with steamed milk served in a 3.5oz glass tumbler.

LATTE (6)

Espresso with silky steamed milk. Drink size of 10-12oz results in a more muted coffee flavour than a flat white.

BREW METHODS

FRENCH PRESS/ CAFETIERE (7)

Freshly ground beans and hot water are brewed together in the base of the cafetiere for 3-4 minutes. Any foam is then removed from the top, the filter is plunged and it's ready to pour.

SYPHON

Creating steam in the bottom chamber forces and keeps water in the top chamber where the ground coffee is added. When the brewing process is complete, the heat source is turned off and the brewed coffee drops through a filter back into the bottom.

V60 (8)

An individual pourover method that's placed over a cup. A choice of filter (paper, metal or cloth) is placed in the funnel of the V60, freshly ground coffee added and hot water poured over. The coffee drips into the cup.

AEROPRESS (9)

Coffee is placed in the top chamber and hot water added. After 2 minutes of brewing the AeroPress is slowly plunged. Pressure forces the steeped liquid through the filter and into a cup.

CHEMEX (10)

Filter paper is placed in the funnel of the Chemex, ground coffee is added and hot water poured over. After steeping, the filter and coffee grounds are removed, leaving the coffee ready to pour.

COLD BREW

Ground coffee is steeped in cold water for anything between 15-20 hours to create a concentrate which is diluted to taste and served chilled.

NITRO COLD BREW

Cold brew infused with nitrogen and pulled through a draught tap to add creaminess.

BREW METHODS

7

8

9

10

BREAKFAST AND BRUNCH

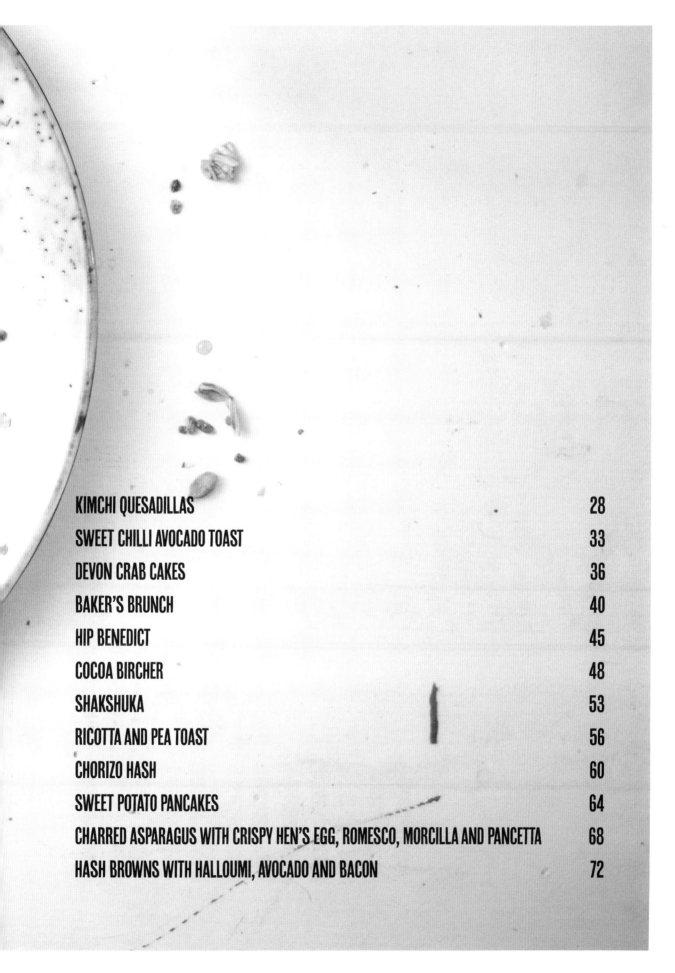

BRAZIER COFFEE ROASTERS

Wellington, Somerset

A hundred years ago, this 19th-century red brick warehouse in Wellington was the site of cloth production for World War I.

However since 2017, Puttee House has been home to pioneering coffee roastery Brazier and its on-site cafe and espresso bar.

Aussie owner Claire and British husband Tom recreate antipodean coffee culture in cool surroundings for the loyal band of locals who swing by for breakfast, lunch and coffee.

Recipe
KIMCHI QUESADILLAS

KIMCHI QUESADILLAS

Recipe by Steven Kiernan of Brazier Coffee Roasters

Serves **4 (makes one large jar of kimchi)**

Preparation time **2-5 days**

Assembly time **5 minutes**

For the kimchi

Japanese cabbage 1, cut into 5cm strips

Kosher salt 100g

Carrots 3, thinly sliced

Daikon radish 1 large, thinly sliced

Spring onions 2 bunches, cut into 2.5cm pieces

Garlic 2 tbsp, minced

Ginger 2 tbsp, minced

Korean red pepper flakes 4 tbsp

For the quesadillas

Tortillas 4

Avocados 2 smashed, to serve

Vegan cheese or feta to serve

Refried black beans to serve

Tomato salsa to serve

1. **For the kimchi:** place the cabbage in a large bowl and sprinkle with salt. Mix thoroughly with your hands, using gloves if preferred. Place a heavy pot on top with weights and allow the cabbage to sit for 1-2 hours until wilted and water is released.

2. Discard the water and rinse the cabbage 2-3 times until the salt is removed. Allow to drain in a colander for 15-20 minutes.

3. Combine the cabbage with the remaining kimchi ingredients (except the pepper flakes) and mix. Using gloves, add the red pepper flakes and rub into the mixture.

4. Once combined, place mixture in a jar, pressing down and packing tightly so that it's submerged in its own liquid. Place top on the jar and leave at room temperature for 2-5 days. Store the jar on a plate as the mixture may bubble over while fermenting.

5. Each day of fermentation, remove the lid to release gases and press down the mixture to keep it submerged. Taste it every day to assess the flavour. Once you're happy, store it in the fridge.

6. **To assemble the quesadillas:** toast a tortilla and layer generously with kimchi, smashed avocado, cheese, refried black beans and tomato salsa.

'Kimchi can elevate lots of dishes: try it stirred through scrambled eggs'

COFFEE PAIRING

*Brazier Coffee Roasters
Finca Liquidambar*

Chemex

PLAYLIST PAIRING

I Need Never Get Old

**Nathaniel Rateliff &
The Night Sweats**

BLOC

Holmfirth, West Yorkshire

Whether you're a member of the smashed avo and egg fraternity, more of a manchego and chorizo fan or a straight up peanut butter purist, you'll find something tasty on toast at this basilica to grilled bread.

Other than the Dark Woods coffee and collection of Canton teas, almost everything at the contemporary cafe is served via the king of carbs. Flavour mash-ups from the creative bunch in the kitchen change regularly, depending on the latest haul from local producers, so there's always something seasonal to get stuck into.

Recipe
SWEET CHILLI AVOCADO TOAST

SWEET CHILLI AVOCADO TOAST

Recipe by Meg Beever, Ellie Schofield and Rachel Raynes of Bloc

Serves **4**

Preparation time **10 minutes**

Cooking time **5 minutes**

For the sweet chilli salsa

Cucumber ½,
deseeded and cubed

Fresh mint a handful, washed
and chopped

Sweet chilli sauce 250g

Halloumi 250g, cut
into 8 slices

Oil 1 tbsp

Free-range eggs 4

Sourdough 4 slices, toasted

Ripe avocados 2, sliced
and mashed

Cracked black pepper to serve

Chilli flakes to serve

Pea shoots to garnish

1. **For the sweet chilli salsa:** combine the cucumber, mint and sweet chilli sauce in a bowl.

2. In a lightly-oiled large frying pan, fry the halloumi slices for 1-2 minutes on each side until golden. Remove from the pan.

3. Add the oil to the pan and, once hot, fry the eggs sunny-side up.

4. **To assemble:** pop the toasted sourdough on a plate, top with avocado, 2 slices of halloumi and a fried egg. Season the egg with cracked black pepper, chilli flakes and dress with pea shoots. Serve the sweet chilli salsa on the side.

'Use egg rings in the frying pan for perfect fried eggs'

COFFEE PAIRING

Dark Woods Coffee
Flat White

PLAYLIST PAIRING

Rapper's Delight
The Sugarhill Gang

JOHNS OF INSTOW AND APPLEDORE

North Devon

For almost a century locals have made a beeline for Johns for its cornucopia of South West produce and deli delights. And, since the family-owned stores and cafes (there's one of each on either side of the estuary at Instow and Appledore) teamed up with Roastworks at the start of 2018, it's also where they head for a great cup of coffee.

After sipping a velvety flat white in the light 'n' bright cafes, visitors are usually tempted to stick around for lunch thanks to Johns' menu of homemade and locally-sourced dishes. Dorset smoked kippers, Devon cheese and local sausages all feature on a line-up which satisfies wandering appetites from daybreak through to afternoon tea.

Recipe
DEVON CRAB CAKES

DEVON CRAB CAKES

Recipe by Anthony and Sue Johns of Johns of Instow and Appledore

Serves **4**

Preparation time **10 minutes**

Cooking time **20 minutes**

For the crab cakes

Fresh white and brown
crab meat 450g

Mayonnaise 1½ tbsp

Dijon mustard 1½ tsp

Chipotle sauce 1 tbsp

Free-range egg 1, beaten

Gluten-free panko
breadcrumbs 4 tbsp

Spring onions 1 bunch,
finely chopped

Olive oil spray

Free-range eggs 4

White wine
vinegar a splash

Spinach 4 handfuls,
washed and dried

Chilli flakes 4 pinches

1. Preheat the oven to 180°c / gas 4.

2. **For the crab cakes:** place the crab meat, mayonnaise, mustard, chipotle sauce, egg, 2 tbsp of breadcrumbs and spring onions in a large bowl and combine.

3. Divide the crab mix into 4 equal portions, roll into balls and shape into patties approximately 10cm in diameter.

4. Coat the patties in the remaining breadcrumbs until evenly covered. Spray with the olive oil, place on a tray and bake in the preheated oven for 20 minutes.

5. 5 minutes before removing the crab cakes, poach the eggs in a pan of simmering water with a splash of white wine vinegar for 4 minutes.

6. **To assemble:** dress the plate with spinach, add the crab cake with a poached egg on top and sprinkle with chilli flakes.

`Use an oil spray to get an even coating on the crab cakes`

COFFEE PAIRING
Roastworks Coffee Co
Flat White

PLAYLIST PAIRING
Let's Do It,
Let's Fall In Love
Ella Fitzgerald

URSA MINOR

Ballycastle, Northern Ireland

Outgrowing the original Ursa Minor Bakehouse, Ciara Ohartghaile and co moved to their current Ballycastle bakery and coffee shop at the start of 2017.

Hand-shaped sourdough loaves baked using traditional techniques are the daily bread at this coastal hangout, though the dedicated team also crack out an incredible line-up of sweet bakes and brunch dishes, as well as a killer cup of speciality coffee.

Recipe
BAKER'S BRUNCH

BAKER'S BRUNCH

Recipe by Ciara Ohartghaile of Ursa Minor

Serves **2**

Preparation time **20 minutes**

Cooking time **10 minutes**

For the hummus

Chickpeas 1 can, drained

Tahini 1 tbsp

Olive oil 3 tbsp

Ground cumin 1 tsp

Salt large pinch

Garlic clove 1, chopped

Lemon ½, juice

For the granola

Oats large handful

Buckwheat 2 tbsp

Seeds 1 tbsp

Tamari 2 tbsp

Rapeseed oil 4 tbsp

For the pesto

Veg tops (kale or soft green herbs) large handful

Nuts (such as walnuts and cashews) 2 tbsp

Nutritional yeast 2 tbsp

Olive oil 4 tbsp

Lemon ½, juice

Garlic clove 1, chopped

Salt and pepper to taste

Olive oil 1 tbsp

Tomatoes 4, cut into large chunks

Courgette 1, ribboned with a peeler

Sourdough bread 2 slices, toasted

1. **For the hummus:** put all of the ingredients into a food processor and blend until it becomes a paste, add water slowly and continue to blend until smooth. Check seasoning and adjust if needed.

2. **For the granola:** put all of the ingredients in a frying pan and mix together so everything is coated in the oil and tamari. Toast over a medium heat, stirring regularly to avoid burning, for around 5 minutes. Remove from heat and set aside.

3. **For the pesto:** put all of the ingredients into a food processor and blend until smooth. Check and adjust seasoning.

4. Heat the oil in a pan, add tomatoes and courgette and cook for around 5-8 minutes, stirring every so often.

5. **To assemble:** spread the hummus on the toast, top with the warmed tomato and courgette, then the pesto and granola and drizzle with a little olive oil.

COFFEE PAIRING

Koppi Ethiopian

Chemex

PLAYLIST PAIRING

Ephrata

Joshua Burnside

'Sprinkle the leftover granola on salads and savoury dishes'

THE FLOWER CUP

Chester, Cheshire

Guaranteed to earn a lot of love on the 'gram, The Flower Cup's slick set-up (combining kick-ass coffee, dreamy all-day brunch dishes and an in-house flower shop) means the only filter you'll need at this picture-worthy spot comes via a Clever Dripper.

Knowledgeable baristas work with single origin beans from Liverpool's Neighbourhood Coffee, and are as committed to crafting excellent espresso-based brews as they are about tending to the plants that fill this urban jungle.

Recipe
HIP BENEDICT

HIP BENEDICT

Recipe by Joe Stock of The Flower Cup

Serves **2**

Preparation time **5 minutes**

Cooking time **15 minutes**

For the avocado hollandaise

Avocado 1, skinned
and destoned

Olive oil 2 tbsp

Lemon juice 2 tbsp

White wine vinegar 1 tbsp

Salt and pepper to season

Streaky bacon 4 rashers

Free-range eggs 2

For the sriracha mayo

Mayonnaise 2 tbsp

Sriracha 1 tsp

Sourdough 2 slices, toasted

Rocket

1. **For the avocado hollandaise:** put the avocado, olive oil, lemon juice, vinegar and salt and pepper in a food processor and blend until smooth.

2. Place the bacon on a tray and grill until crispy. Poach the eggs in barely-simmering water for 3-5 minutes until cooked on the outside and soft in the middle.

3. **For the sriracha mayo:** combine the mayonnaise and the sriracha.

4. **To assemble:** drizzle the sriracha mayo on the toasted sourdough, then add the poached egg and crispy bacon. Pour avocado hollandaise over the top then dress with rocket.

'Add a sprinkle of chilli flakes for a fiery hit'

COFFEE PAIRING

Neighbourhood Coffee

Clever Dripper

PLAYLIST PAIRING

Sexual Healing

Hot 8 Brass Band

MERAKI COFFEE COMPANY

Woolacombe, North Devon

This side-street gem is just a salty-haired dash from Woolacombe's sandy shore. Self-taught baristas and owners Anthony Merret and Rohan Molligoda took over the former gallery at the start of 2018 and wasted no time in transforming the space into an easy-going coffee shop where sea foam-frolickers fill up on homemade specials and tourists escape the bustle for a quality caffeine fix.

When he's not bobbing about in the surf, you'll find Anthony slinging Devon Coffee Company espresso at the slick Astoria Storm machine which crowns the stainless-steel-top bar.

Recipe
COCOA BIRCHER

COCOA BIRCHER

Recipe by Anthony Merret of Meraki Coffee Company

Serves **1**

Preparation time **10 minutes (plus overnight soaking)**

Almond milk 200ml

Banana 1, peeled

Peanut butter 1 tsp

Maple syrup 15g

Cocoa powder 10g

Oats 100g

Dark chocolate 2 squares

Hazelnuts a handful, crushed

Raspberries 6

Desiccated coconut 1 tsp

1. Put the almond milk, banana, peanut butter, maple syrup and cocoa into a blender and blitz until smooth.

2. Pour the mix into an airtight container, add the oats and combine.

3. Place the container in the fridge and leave the oats to soak overnight.

4. The next day, spoon the mixture into a bowl. Grate dark chocolate over the top and then sprinkle with crushed hazelnuts, raspberries and coconut.

'Prep a big batch of the bircher - it will keep in the fridge for up to five days'

COFFEE PAIRING

The Devon Coffee Company
Cappuccino

PLAYLIST PAIRING

Everyday People
Sly And The Family Stone

LAYNES ESPRESSO

Leeds, West Yorkshire

The first call on any caffeine tour of Leeds, this northern coffee scene pioneer is just seconds from the train station and has welcomed visitors to the city with a stellar cup since 2011.

Scores of speciality pilgrims pile in to sample the coffee offering and newly pimped menus. On weekends you'll find the place abuzz with friends debriefing over braised beans and cornbread, and speciality geeks getting their fill of savoury buckwheat pancakes.

Recipe
SHAKSHUKA

SHAKSHUKA

Recipe by Vic Rees of Laynes Espresso

Serves **4**

Preparation time **10 minutes**

Cooking time **35 minutes**

Red peppers 2, thinly sliced

Red onion 1, thinly sliced

Garlic 3 cloves, crushed

Olive oil 2 tbsp

White onion 1, diced

Celery 3 sticks, diced

Ground cumin 1 tbsp

Smoked paprika 1 tbsp

Tomato puree 1 tbsp

Plum tomatoes 2 tins

Harissa paste 1 tsp

Sugar a pinch

Salt and pepper to taste

Red wine vinegar a splash

Free-range eggs 4 large

To serve

Sumac

Fresh herbs such as coriander and dill

Flatbreads

1. Place the red pepper and red onion on a baking tray and grill until slightly charred.

2. Put a large frying pan on a low heat on the hob and gently poach the garlic in the oil for around 5 minutes. Then remove from the pan and put aside.

3. Turn the heat up to medium and add the white onion and celery. Once they've softened, add the charred red pepper and red onion to the pan. Then add the cumin, paprika and puree and stir constantly for 2-3 minutes, before adding the tinned tomatoes and harissa. Finally, pour in half a tin of water and stir.

4. Leave the sauce to cook in a pan over a gentle heat for 35-40 minutes, adding more water if it becomes too thick.

5. Sample the sauce and add sugar, salt, pepper, red wine vinegar and additional harissa to taste.

6. Once you're happy with the sauce, make four wells in it (still in the pan) and crack in the eggs. Cover with a lid or foil and cook until the whites are just done and the yolks runny.

'Serve with *sumac*, chopped herbs and toasted flatbread'

COFFEE PAIRING

Square Mile natural process single origin

Pourover

PLAYLIST PAIRING

SoWhat

Dil Withers

ORIGIN COFFEE ROASTERS

Penryn, Cornwall

Origin's outpost at The Warehouse in Penryn is the latest addition to its boutique collection of speciality coffee shops in Cornwall and London.

Visiting coffee fiends can explore a selection of beans which have been roasted on two Loring Smart Roasts at Origin's Helston HQ.

The coffee is then crafted into outstanding cups by committed baristas whose raison d'être is to welcome, educate and help customers. The food's pretty good too.

Recipe
RICOTTA AND PEA TOAST

RICOTTA AND PEA TOAST

Recipe by Jenn Wickings of Origin Coffee Roasters

Serves **1**

Preparation time **10 minutes**

Cooking time **5 minutes**

Ricotta 4 tbsp

Honey 1 tsp

Lemon 1, juice and zest

Fresh dill 1 bunch, roughly chopped

Fresh peas 1 handful

Fresh mint 1 bunch, roughly chopped

Extra virgin olive oil

Sunflower and pumpkin seeds 1 tbsp

Miso paste ½ tsp

Sourdough 1 slice, toasted

Watercress 1 handful

Micro coriander a pinch

Radishes 3, finely sliced

Cornish Sea Salt and cracked black pepper to season

1. Whip together the ricotta, honey, half the lemon juice and zest and the dill.

2. Steam the peas for 2-3 minutes until cooked. Tip into a small bowl, then add the mint and a drizzle of olive oil.

3. Pour a tablespoon of olive oil into a small non-stick frying pan over a medium heat, then add the sunflower seeds, pumpkin seeds and miso paste. Stir and remove from the heat when the seeds begin to crackle.

4. Spread a thick layer of the ricotta mixture onto the toasted sourdough.

5. Sprinkle the peas, watercress, micro coriander, radishes and toasted seeds over the top. Then squeeze the rest of the lemon juice over it all. Season to taste.

'We use sourdough from Da Bara Bakery in Truro'

COFFEE PAIRING

Origin Coffee Roasters
San Fermin

Pourover

PLAYLIST PAIRING

Into The Mystic

Van Morrison

GRIND & TAMP

Ramsbottom, Greater Manchester

Guest coffees take centre stage at this popular speciality hangout in the heart of Ramsbottom.

Headline spots on its six-strong bill of beans go to Lancaster's Atkinsons, Leeds' North Star and London's Square Mile, while a chorus of guest roasters also get their monthly moment in the spotlight.

But it's not only the coffee that inspires comeback tours at this charming old brick building: the brunch and lunch menus change weekly and stalwarts like the sausage and egg muffin and chorizo hash have amassed their own fanbase.

Recipe
CHORIZO HASH

CHORIZO HASH

Recipe by Adrian Barratt-Smith of Grind & Tamp

Serves **2**

Preparation time **30-35 minutes**

Cooking time **10 minutes**

For the hash
Red pepper 1

Olive oil 2 tbsp

Red onion 1, sliced

Chorizo picante 100g, sliced

Potatoes 200g, cooked
and crushed

Carrots 50g, diced and cooked

Celeriac 50g, diced and cooked

Smoked paprika 1 tsp

Cayenne pepper a pinch

Salt and pepper to season

For the chipotle yogurt
Natural yogurt 2 tbsp

Chipotle sauce ¼ tsp

Tomato 1, halved

Free-range eggs 2

Wild rocket leaves a handful

Balsamic vinegar 2 tbsp

Olive oil a drizzle

1. **For the hash:** grill the whole red pepper under a high heat until it blisters and starts to char. Remove and place it in a sealed plastic bag. Once cool, peel to remove the skin, then slice open to remove the seeds and stalk. Slice the pepper flesh into strips.

2. In a large pan, heat the oil over a medium heat. Add the onion and soften for 3-4 minutes. Add the chorizo and continue to cook until the oils begin to release.

3. Add the cooked potatoes, carrot, celeriac and red pepper to the pan and combine. Add the smoked paprika, cayenne, salt and pepper. Keep the ingredients moving in the pan with a wooden spoon and cook for around 8 minutes.

4. **For the chipotle yogurt:** combine the yogurt and chipotle sauce until smooth.

5. Season the tomato with salt and pepper and grill under a medium heat. Once blistered, keep warm until ready to serve.

6. In a hot pan, fry the eggs sunny-side up.

7. Dress the rocket with olive oil and balsamic vinegar.

8. **To assemble:** stack the hash on a warm plate and top with a fried egg. Serve with grilled tomato, rocket and a good dollop of the chipotle yogurt.

'Make it veggie by swapping the chorizo for griddled aubergine or halloumi'

COFFEE PAIRING

Grind & Tamp

24-Hour Cold Brew

PLAYLIST PAIRING

Shotgun

George Ezra

FOODSTORY

Aberdeen, Scotland

This particular Foodstory is a little like a fairytale. There were hopes (of opening a fantastic cafe), there was jeopardy (when the lease taken out on the original building turned out to be worthless), true love (finding the current premises) and a dream come true (the plan worked, customers loved it and Foodstory has grown beyond the team's wildest dreams).

The next chapter saw the launch of a wholefoods shop upstairs, while downstairs the kitchen has been expanded to make the most of the vibrant veggie and vegan food offering. Now that's a happy ending.

Recipe
SWEET POTATO PANCAKES

SWEET POTATO PANCAKES

Recipe by Sara Kindness of Foodstory

Serves **6**

Preparation time **30 minutes**

Cooking time **20 minutes**

For the pancakes

Plain gluten-free flour 425g

Gluten-free baking
powder 1½ tsp

Cinnamon 1½ tsp

Ground nutmeg ¼ tsp

Ground ginger ¼ tsp

Ground cardamom ¼ tsp

Salt a pinch

Sweet potato puree 100ml

Rice malt extract 1 tbsp
(alternatively, use maple syrup)

Vanilla extract 1 tsp

Almond milk 400ml

Coconut oil 3 tbsp

Granola and fruit to serve

Maple syrup to drizzle

1. **For the pancakes:** put the flour, baking powder, cinnamon, nutmeg, ginger, cardamom and salt in a large mixing bowl and combine.

2. Make the sweet potato puree by roasting or microwaving the sweet potatoes in their skins and mashing or squeezing out the flesh when cooked.

3. Mix the sweet potato with the rice malt extract and vanilla extract, then add to the dry ingredients and combine everything.

4. Gradually add the almond milk until the pancake batter reaches a thick, syrupy texture.

5. Heat the coconut oil in a large frying pan. Once melted, carefully pour a portion of the batter into the centre.

6. Cook for 2-3 minutes before flipping and cooking for a further 2-3 minutes on the other side.

7. **To assemble:** serve the pancakes in a stack with granola, fresh fruit such as berries and apple plus a drizzle of maple syrup.

Caramelised apples make a great addition to the sprinkle of granola and berries

COFFEE PAIRING

*Dear Green Colombian
single origin*

Pourover

PLAYLIST PAIRING

On A Rooftop

Anna Mieke

TEABREW TEA CO. LOOSE

CHAI LATTE £2.⁹⁵

KOKOA COLLECTION HOT

WHITE · 58% SMOOTH

ADO CREAM & MARSHM

KIDS   MINI HOT CHOC

BABY FLUFF .60P   · STE

TINCAN COFFEE CO.

Bristol, South West

Tincan's roots snake back to 2011, when it began serving speciality brews to caffeine-craving, wellie-clad festival-goers from its fleet of roving coffee trucks.

The mobile espresso bars continue to thrive but the Tincan brand has also firmly cemented itself as a less moveable feast at its Southville and Bishopston cafes, where it has brewed up a loyal following for the revolving line-up of guest beans and brunch specials.

Recipe
CHARRED ASPARAGUS WITH CRISPY HEN'S EGG, ROMESCO, MORCILLA AND PANCETTA

CHARRED ASPARAGUS WITH CRISPY HEN'S EGG, ROMESCO, MORCILLA AND PANCETTA

Recipe by Tincan Coffee Co.

Serves **1**

Preparation time **10 minutes**

Cooking time **10 minutes**

For the eggs

Free-range eggs 2 medium, whole

Plain flour 30g

Free-range egg 1, beaten

Panko breadcrumbs 30g

For the romesco

Blanched almonds 50g

Ripe tomatoes 250g

Nora peppers 6, tinned (pre-charred)

Stale bread 3 slices

Garlic 1 clove, crushed

Good quality olive oil 50ml

Sherry vinegar 25ml

Morcilla 50g, sliced

Smoked pancetta 3 slices

Wye Valley asparagus 4 spears, washed and ends removed

Oil for frying

Watercress or pea shoots to garnish

1. **For the eggs:** bring a pan of water to the boil. Place the whole eggs in the water with a slotted spoon and cook for 6 minutes. Remove them from the pan and plunge into a bowl of iced water.

2. Once the whole eggs are cool, remove their shells. Roll them in the flour, then the beaten egg and finally the breadcrumbs. Fry in oil until golden.

3. **For the romesco:** toast the almonds in a pan until golden. Move to one side of the pan and add the tomatoes until charred. Add this to a blender with the rest of the romesco ingredients and blitz until coarse.

4. Fry the morcilla and pancetta slices in 1 tbsp of oil until crispy. In a cast iron pan, char the asparagus until blackened on one side and tender to the bite.

5. **To assemble:** serve the asparagus with the crispy eggs, fried morcilla and pancetta, pea shoots or watercress and a drizzle of romesco.

COFFEE PAIRING

Extract El Guayabito

Cortado

PLAYLIST PAIRING

Captain Brunch

Czarface & MF Doom

'Asparagus out of season? Use cavolo nero or rainbow chard instead'

HAYSTACK

Swansea, South Wales

With its 20ft mural extolling the life-enhancing virtues of brunch, this fresher on the Swansea speciality scene is pretty hard to miss.

Haystack owners Liam and Beth secured their sweet corner spot in spring 2018 and took inspiration from Beth's rural upbringing to create a sociable cafe space serving the best of South Wales' produce.

Having spent time in London before returning to Swansea, the couple wanted to pair their epic brunch offering with city-standard coffee. Happily, locally-roasted Coaltown Coffee beans provide the perfect blend of third-wave quality and Welsh locality.

Recipe
HASH BROWNS WITH HALLOUMI, AVOCADO AND BACON

HASH BROWNS WITH HALLOUMI, AVOCADO AND BACON

Recipe by Bethan Roberts of Haystack

Serves **4**

Preparation time **10 minutes**

Cook time **10 minutes**

For the hash browns

Baking potatoes 3, peeled and grated

Plain flour 1 tbsp

Free-range egg 1, large

Salt and pepper to season

Oil 1 tbsp

Back bacon 4 rashers

Halloumi 250g, sliced

Ripe avocados 2, smashed

Sriracha to serve

1. **For the hash browns:** combine the potato, flour and egg in a large bowl and season with salt and pepper. Shape the mix into 8 disk-shaped patties and refrigerate for 30 minutes.

2. Heat the oil in a large pan and when hot add the hash browns. Shallow fry for 4 minutes before flipping and cooking for a further 4 minutes or until golden brown.

3. Fry the bacon until crisp then drain on kitchen roll. Fry the halloumi slices until golden brown in colour.

4. **To assemble:** place a hash brown on each plate and then stack with smashed avocado, bacon, halloumi and then another hash brown. Season with salt and pepper and drizzle with sriracha sauce.

'Go all out and add a couple of poached eggs for the *heartiest weekend* feed'

COFFEE PAIRING

Coaltown Coffee Roasters
Brazilian espresso

Cortado

PLAYLIST PAIRING

Glitter & Gold

Barns Courtney

LUNCH AND SUPPER

CAIRNGORM COFFEE

Edinburgh, Scotland

With a monthly-changing espresso and weekly single origin on batch brew, every trip to Cairngorm's outposts on Melville Place and Frederick Street offer something novel for the seasoned coffee swigger.

The caffeine is in constant development as owner Robi recently moved on from buying in bronzed beans to roasting his own.

Unctuous grilled cheese sandwiches, slick decor and a sociable vibe are the additional perks of a trip to either of Cairngorm's contemporary coffee shops and have made them a firm fave with locals and tourists alike.

Recipe
TERIYAKI JACKFRUIT

TERIYAKI JACKFRUIT WITH RED CABBAGE AND CARROT SLAW

Recipe by Dawn Wong of Cairngorm Coffee

Serves **2**

Preparation time **20 minutes**

Cooking time **20 minutes**

For the red cabbage and carrot slaw

Red cabbage 100g, thinly sliced

Carrot 1 medium, thinly sliced

Olive oil 1 tsp

Rice wine vinegar 2 tbsp

Salt ½ tsp

For the teriyaki jackfruit

Jackfruit in brine or water 1 can, drained and broken into chunks

Garlic 2 cloves, minced

Fresh ginger 1 tsp, minced

Sesame oil 1 tbsp

Brown sugar 3 tbsp

Soy sauce 60ml

Mirin 1 tsp

Rice wine vinegar 1 tsp

White sesame seeds 1 tsp, toasted

Black sesame seeds 1 tsp, toasted

For the avocado

Avocado 1, peeled and destoned

Lime ½, juice

Rye bread rolls 2, to serve

1. **For the red cabbage and carrot slaw:** place all of the ingredients in a bowl and massage the wet ingredients into the vegetables. Leave the vegetables for a few minutes to soften. Taste and add more vinegar or salt if needed.

2. **For the teriyaki jackfruit:** place the large chunks in a pan with the olive oil and sauté over a medium heat. Stir occasionally until golden. Set aside.

3. Put the garlic, ginger, sesame oil, brown sugar, soy sauce, mirin and vinegar in a pan. Add the jackfruit and simmer over a medium heat until the sauce reduces to a glaze. Remove from the heat and allow to cool.

4. Sprinkle in the sesame seeds and stir with a wooden spoon, using the back of the spoon to break up the jackfruit.

5. **For the avocado:** smash the avocado with the back of a fork and drizzle with the lime juice.

6. **To assemble:** slice the roll in half. On the bottom half layer the avocado, slaw and finish with the jackfruit. Place the other half of the roll on top and serve.

COFFEE PAIRING

Rwanda Huye Mountain

Filter

PLAYLIST PAIRING

Pig

This Town Needs Guns

'Dress any **excess avocado** with lime juice to prevent it going brown'

TAMPER COFFEE

Sheffield, South Yorkshire

Switching things up on a regular basis has become a Tamper trademark and kept this Kiwi-inspired eatery ahead of the game since it opened in 2011.

The portfolio is now three-strong and at the Sellers Wheel outpost you'll find a cool polished concrete bar, colourful wall mural and expertly crafted Dark Woods coffee.

The sweetcorn fritters are a staple on both the breakfast and lunch menus here. Pair them with a flat white and a slice of sourdough from sister bakery, The Depot, for a blast of NZ all-day cafe culture.

Recipe
SWEETCORN FRITTERS

'Score an extra hour in bed: make the fritters the day before'

COFFEE PAIRING

Dark Woods

Flat White

PLAYLIST PAIRING

Move On Up

Curtis Mayfield

SWEETCORN FRITTERS WITH BEETROOT TWO WAYS AND POACHED EGG

Recipe by Thomas Donald of Tamper Coffee

Serves **2**

Preparation time **25-30 minutes**

Cooking time **10 minutes**

For the sweetcorn fritters
Sweetcorn 320g (2 tins, drained)
Free-range eggs 2
Garlic 1 clove, chopped
Paprika 1 tsp
Gram flour 90g, sieved
Baking powder 1 tsp
Chervil small bunch, chopped
Salt and pepper to season

For the crushed beetroot
Cooked beetroot 3
Olive oil 1 tbsp
Dill small bunch, chopped
Chervil small bunch, chopped
Salt and pepper to season

For the beetroot yogurt
Cooked beetroot 1
Natural yogurt 50g
Crème fraîche 50g

For the sweet chilli cucumber
Sweet chilli sauce 100ml
Cucumber ¼, deseeded and finely diced

Olive oil 2 tbsp
Butter 15g
White wine vinegar a splash
Free-range eggs 2

1. *For the sweetcorn fritters:* tip 1 tin of sweetcorn into a blender with the eggs, garlic and paprika. Blend until nearly smooth and then transfer to a large bowl. Add the other tin of sweetcorn to the mixture, along with the flour, baking powder and chervil. Fold the mixture until fully combined, then refrigerate to firm up.

2. *For the crushed beetroot:* place the beetroot in a blender with the oil and pulse until it forms a thick hummus-like consistency. Transfer to a bowl, add the herbs and season.

3. *For the beetroot yogurt:* add the beetroot and yogurt to a blender and blitz until completely smooth. Transfer to a bowl and whisk in the crème fraîche. Keep in the fridge until ready to serve.

4. *For the sweet chilli cucumber:* combine the sweet chilli sauce and cucumber and refrigerate until ready to serve.

5. In a large frying pan, heat the olive oil and butter. Once the butter foams, separate the fritter mix into 4 and spoon into the pan. Cook on a medium heat for 4-5 minutes before flipping. Lightly press the fritters with a spatula and cook for a further 4-5 minutes.

6. Poach the eggs in a small pan of water with a splash of white wine vinegar over a low heat.

7. *To assemble:* when everything is ready, spoon the beetroot yogurt onto a plate. Place the two fritters on top, add the sweet chilli cucumber and a spoonful of crushed beetroot and top with a poached egg.

HAPTIK

Newtownards, Northern Ireland

Haptik's husband and wife team, Jonathan and Rachel McBride, blend their passions for speciality coffee, contemporary art, food and community at their Newtownards townhouse cafe.

The ground floor is dedicated to top-notch coffee and feasts of homemade fodder. Upstairs, Rachel curates a kaleidoscope of contemporary pieces from local artists in the gallery space.

This year, Haptik's line-up of seasonal themed supper clubs have become a highlight in the local foodie calendar.

Recipe
LIGHT SEAFOOD CHOWDER

LIGHT SEAFOOD CHOWDER

Recipe by Kenton Menown of Haptik

Serves **4-6**

Preparation time **15 minutes**

Cooking time **30 minutes**

For the chowder

Olive oil 1 tbsp

Onion 1, finely chopped

Leek 1, finely sliced

Carrots 3 (2 diced, 1 grated)

Celery sticks 2, sliced

Baby potatoes 250g, quartered

Garlic cloves 2 large,
finely chopped

Cayenne pepper ½ tsp

Smoked paprika 1 tsp

Chicken stock 600ml

Salt and pepper a pinch

Fish pie mix 400g (equal
quantities of white fish,
smoked white fish and salmon)

King prawns 180g, uncooked
and frozen

Whole milk 250ml

Parsley a small bunch

Dill chopped

Scallions (spring onions)
1 bunch, sliced

Lemon 1, quartered

1. Heat the oil in a large pan over a medium heat. Add the onion and leek and sauté for 4-5 minutes until the onion begins to turn transparent.

2. Add the carrots, celery and potatoes. Mix well and cook for a further 10 minutes until the vegetables begin to soften.

3. Turn up the heat, add the garlic and fry for 1 minute, followed by the cayenne pepper and smoked paprika. Stir constantly to release the oils from the spices without burning them.

4. Pour in the chicken stock and season with salt and pepper. Boil for 10 minutes or until the potatoes are soft.

5. Add the fish mix and prawns, then turn down the heat to a simmer for a further 3-5 minutes. Take care not to overcook the fish.

6. Remove the chowder from the heat and allow to cool slightly. Add the milk and parsley and stir gently to avoid breaking up the fish.

7. Serve sprinkled with chopped dill and scallions in a warm bowl with a wedge of lemon.

COFFEE PAIRING

Bailies Honduras Las Flores
Filter

PLAYLIST PAIRING

Stare Too Long
Corrosion Of Conformity

'For a more intense flavour, add sliced bacon to the pan when fryig the onion'

CAFE SIA

Isle of Skye, Scotland

Specialising in house-roasted coffee and wood-fired pizza (cooked in an oven that owner Tom drove home to Skye from Pisa), it's no surprise that Cafe Sia is usually rammed.

Once you're over the bridge and onto Skye, you're just a hop, skip and a jump from the diner-style cafe. Get here early if you want to nab a table, or visit mid-morning for a decent flattie and hang until the pizza oven is fired up.

Recipe
DEAMHAN PIZZA

DEAMHAN PIZZA

Recipe by Karen Copeland of Cafe Sia

Makes **4 pizzas**

Preparation time **1–1½ hours**

Cooking time **15 minutes**

For the dough

Dried yeast 1 dsp

Table salt 1 tsp

Caster sugar 1 tsp

Olive oil 100ml

Water 600ml at approx 37°c

Strong bread flour (pizza flour or gluten-free flour also work) 1kg

For the sauce

Tomato paste 200g

Chopped tomatoes 400g tin

Garlic cloves 2, crushed

Italian seasoning 1 tsp

Caster sugar 1 tsp

Salt and black pepper a pinch

For the topping

Red peppers 2, sliced

Olive oil a drizzle

Salt and pepper to season

Venison salami (or Italian salami) 20-25 slices

Mozzarella 400g, grated

For the chilli oil

Scotch bonnet chillies (or any strong chillies) 2-3

Olive oil 175ml

1. **For the dough:** put the yeast, salt, sugar, oil and water in a mixer. Slowly add the flour until a soft dough forms around the hook attachment. Remove and knead lightly on a floured surface. Place in a bowl, cover with clingfilm and put in a warm area for around an hour until it doubles in size.

2. **For the sauce:** put all the ingredients in a blender and blitz until smooth.

3. **For the topping:** drizzle the red peppers with oil, season with salt and pepper, then roast at 180°c / gas 4 for 5 minutes.

4. **For the chilli oil:** mix the chillies and olive oil in a blender.

5. Heat the oven to 200°c / gas 6. Split the dough into 4 balls and roll out to a circular base, then place on a pre-oiled tray, spreading the dough to the edges. Cook for 5 minutes, then turn over and cook for another 5 minutes.

6. Spread the sauce evenly over the base and add the roasted peppers and salami. Top with the mozzarella and chilli oil, then cook for a further 5 minutes, keeping a close eye to make sure it doesn't burn.

COFFEE PAIRING

Skye Roastery
Ethiopian single origin

Espresso

PLAYLIST PAIRING

Highway To Hell

AC/DC

'Can't stand the heat?
Ditch the chilli oil and drizzle with balsamic glaze'

PROVIDERO TEA & COFFEE HOUSE

Llandudno, North Wales

A flurry of start-ups followed Jon Hughes' lead when he chose Upper Mostyn Street for Providero's second outpost and kick-started an indie hub just a pebble's skim from Llandudno's shoreside centre.

The sociable space is the uncut version (dubbed 'Big Prov') of the original coffee shop at Llandudno Junction which Jon launched in 2014, and features a meatier food menu and the first Sanremo Opera espresso machine to grace a Welsh bar.

Recipe
BEETROOT AND MINT SMASH

BEETROOT AND MINT SMASH WITH GOAT'S CHEESE AND WALNUTS

Recipe by Evie Hemmings of Providero Tea & Coffee House

Serves **8**

Preparation time **30 minutes**

For the beetroot and mint smash

Tahini 2 tbsp

Lemon 1, juice

Olive oil 2 tbsp

Chickpeas 400g can, drained

Beetroot 500g, pre-cooked

Mint leaves 10, chopped

Salt and pepper to season

Sourdough 8 slices, toasted

Goat's cheese crumbled

Walnuts small handful, broken

Watercress to garnish

Balsamic glaze to drizzle

1. *For the beetroot and mint smash:* put the tahini, lemon juice and olive oil in a blender. Blend until smooth.

2. Add the chickpeas to the blender and mix coarsely, then transfer to a bowl and put aside.

3. Put the beetroot in the blender and coarsely blend before adding the mint, salt and pepper to taste.

4. Combine the beetroot and chickpea mixtures together.

5. *To assemble:* spoon a generous dollop of the smash on a slice of toasted sourdough. Crumble goat's cheese and walnuts over. Place watercress on top and drizzle with balsamic glaze.

'Vegan? Ditch the cheese and add extra nuts, seeds and grapes instead'

COFFEE PAIRING

Heartland Coffi
Malawi Mzuzu

Batch Brew

PLAYLIST PAIRING

90 Degrees

Yazmin Lacey

EXPLODING BAKERY

Exeter, Devon

It's worth catching an early train to Exeter to nab one of the city's best people-watching spots outside Exploding Bakery.

Inside the simply-styled cafe next to Central Station, the bakers' table offers voyeurs an even better snoop at what's going down in the open-plan kitchen. Usually it's the prep of a delicious array of lunch dishes and haul of bakes to scoff with a slow-brewed filter coffee or silky flat white crafted from locally roasted beans.

Recipe
TOMATO AND WATERMELON SALAD

TOMATO AND WATERMELON SALAD

Recipe by Oliver Coysh of Exploding Bakery

Serves **4**

Preparation time **10 minutes**

Vinegar 20ml
Honey 1 tsp
Sea salt 1 tsp
Pepper a good grind
Chilli flakes optional
Red onion 1 small, finely sliced
Heritage tomatoes 500g
Watermelon 500g
Butter beans 400g tin, drained
Cold-pressed rapeseed oil 20ml
Basil 20g
Mint 10g
Fresh bread to serve

1. Pour the vinegar into a large bowl and add the honey, salt, pepper and chilli (if using). Add the sliced onion so it can begin to macerate.

2. Chop the tomatoes in a random fashion with a super sharp knife so the juice and seeds don't fall out. Add to the bowl.

3. Cut the watermelon flesh in a similar fashion and add to the bowl. Next add the drained beans and oil.

4. Chop the herbs, putting small and delicate leaves to one side. Add to the bowl and gently mix everything together.

5. Transfer to a deep platter or bowl and scatter the delicate herbs on top.

6. Drizzle a little more oil on the top and serve with good bread. Use a spoon to serve so you can gather all of the lovely juices at the bottom of the bowl.

This keeps for a couple of days in the fridge and tastes even better on the second day

COFFEE PAIRING

Kenyan Kamwangi

Filter

PLAYLIST PAIRING

Con Todo El Mundo

Khruangbin

BOSTON TEA PARTY

Bath, South West

Bath's Boston Tea Party outposts are caffeine institutions in the speciality savvy city. A lot has happened since the first flat whites were poured at the popular venues and the West Country mini-chain (find 22 of them across the South West, south coast and Midlands) is now a changemaker in the battle against plastic waste. Boston's blanket ban on single-use cups (since June 2018) has already saved tens of thousands of disposables heading to landfill.

It's not just about being eco-warriors though, as serving top-notch coffee in vibrant locations is still priority number one.

Recipe
SPICED LAMB FLATBREAD

SPICED LAMB FLATBREAD

Recipe by Laura Downing of Boston Tea Party

Serves **4**

Preparation time **20-30 minutes**

For the lamb kofte

Lamb mince 500g

Chilli powder 5g

Fresh coriander 20g, chopped

Garam masala 2 tsp

Ground coriander seeds 1 tsp

Ground cumin 1 tsp

Salt and black
pepper to season

Greek yogurt 50g

Extra virgin olive oil 10ml

For the herb salad

Parsley 100g, finely chopped

Coriander 100g, finely chopped

Mint 100g, finely chopped

Radish 100g, finely chopped

Cucumber 100g, finely chopped

Spring onions 50g, finely chopped

Lemon 1, juice

Extra virgin olive oil 20g

For the date jam

Dates 100g

Water 50ml

Greek yogurt 200g

Harissa paste 20g

Sumac 1 tsp

Olive oil

Flatbreads 2, halved and
lightly toasted

Pickled red onion 80g

Toasted sesame seeds 20g

1. **For the lamb kofte:** mix the mince, spices, seasoning and yogurt in a bowl using your hands.

2. Heat the oil in a large frying pan and gently fry the kofte mix until cooked through. Allow to cool and then chop into a rough crumb.

3. **For the herb salad:** combine all of the ingredients in a large bowl.

4. Add the kofte to the herb salad and mix.

5. **For the date jam:** put the dates and water in a blender and blitz until smooth.

6. **To assemble:** place a dollop of yogurt on one side of a shallow bowl and use the back of a spoon to spread the yogurt up one side of the bowl. Place small dots of harissa along the yogurt, sprinkle with sumac and drizzle with olive oil.

7. On the other side of the bowl, place the toasted flatbread half. Spread a generous helping of the date jam on the flatbread and then add a serving of the kofte. Top with pickled red onion and finish with a sprinkle of toasted sesame seeds.

COFFEE PAIRING

*Extract Coffee Roasters
seasonal guest*

Batch Brew

PLAYLIST PAIRING

'Til It's Over

Anderson Paak

'Veggie? Swap the lamb for *crispy fried halloumi*'

THE HEPWORTH CAFE

Wakefield, West Yorkshire

When a *MasterChef* finalist joined forces with one of Leeds' best looking coffee shops, it was clear that the result was going to be deliciously photographable.

Taking over The Hepworth Cafe at Wakefield's award winning museum and art gallery in October 2017, executive chef Chris Hale of Pop Up North and the team behind House of Koko have created a beautiful space to eat, drink and devour a slice of culture.

Recipe
PEACH, PROSCIUTTO AND MOZZARELLA BRUSCHETTA

PEACH, PROSCIUTTO AND MOZZARELLA BRUSCHETTA

Recipe by Chris Hale of The Hepworth Cafe

Serves **2**

Preparation time **10 minutes**

Cooking time **20 minutes**

Peaches 2, destoned and sliced into 6

Salt a pinch

Mint 4 sprigs, finely chopped

Honey 1 tbsp

Rapeseed oil 50ml

Mozzarella 60g, sliced

Prosciutto 4 slices

Sourdough 2 slices, toasted

1. Preheat the oven to 160 °c / gas 3.

2. Season the peaches with salt and roast for 20 minutes.

3. Combine the mint, honey and rapeseed oil in a bowl and whisk to emulsify. Season to taste.

4. Layer the prosciutto, mozzarella and roasted peaches on the toasted sourdough and dress with the mint and honey dressing.

'In late summer, swap the peaches for sticky figs.'

COFFEE PAIRING

North Star Coffee Roasters
Czar Street

Cappuccino

PLAYLIST PAIRING

Waiting On The World
To Change

John Mayer

COMIDA [FOOD]

Kendal, Cumbria

After running their bed and breakfast in Burton-in-Kendal for five years, Alba Basterra and Simon Perkin decided to trade in the towels and turn-downs for tapas, and opened a bar and restaurant on Highgate.

Comida's relaxed vibe reflects the sharing nature of the food. This is a chilled spot in which to chat over a glass of wine or a coffee while taking time to enjoy the pared-back wood and mosaic-tiled space.

Recipe
THE BALL BAGEL

...EL

...a and Simon Perkin of Comida [Food]

⌁ **20 minutes**

ᘈ **1 hour**

For the tomato sauce

Oil 1 tbsp

Onion 1, diced

Garlic 4 cloves, minced

Tomato puree 30g

Fresh tomatoes 400g, diced

Chopped tomatoes 1 tin

Vegetable stock 250ml

Dried oregano 1 tbsp

For the balls (albondigas)

Pork mince 250g

Beef mince 250g

Onion ½, diced

Garlic 1 clove, grated

Free-range egg 1

Stale bread 100g, blitzed

Parsley 1 tbsp, chopped

Olive oil 2 tbsp

Bagels 4

Butter

Manchego cheese

1. **For the tomato sauce:** heat the oil in a large pan. Add the onion and sweat until starting to colour. Add the garlic and fry for 2 minutes. Add the tomato puree and cook for a further 3 minutes.

2. Add the fresh and tinned tomatoes, stock and oregano to the pan and bring to the boil. Reduce the heat and allow to simmer for 40 minutes.

3. **For the albondigas:** combine all of the ingredients (except for the oil) in a large bowl using your hands. Once combined, shape into 50g balls.

4. Heat the oil in a large frying pan and brown off the balls. Add the balls to the tomato sauce and simmer until cooked through.

5. **To assemble:** slice the bagels in half and butter the sliced surfaces. Slice the cooked balls in half and add 4 halves to each bagel. Add a generous spoonful of tomato sauce and a layer of manchego cheese over the meatballs and place under the grill to melt. Put the other half of the bagel on top and serve.

COFFEE PAIRING

Atkinsons Coffee Roasters

Americano

PLAYLIST PAIRING

I'll Still Destroy You

The National

'For a real *garlic hit,* add lashings of good aioli'

BEAN LOVED

Skipton, North Yorkshire

Instead of serving beans from a rotating collection of different roasteries, Bean Loved has gone the simple, purist route and only crafts espresso from Dark Woods roasts.

The team are equally single minded about their food offering, sourcing as many ingredients as possible from within Yorkshire.

Each day, the chefs create hearty soups and seasonal breakfasts from scratch, while cakes are sourced from a line-up of local bakeries.

Recipe
SMOKED CHILLI SALMON SALAD

'To enhance the flavour, add the leftover marinade *to the salmon as it cooks*'

DRINK PAIRING

Sparkling Lemon Verbena And Elderflower Iced Tea

PLAYLIST PAIRING

Heavy, California

Jungle

SMOKED CHILLI SALMON SALAD WITH MANGO, QUINOA, COURGETTE AND RHUBARB

Recipe by Alastair Fox of Bean Loved

Serves **2**

Preparation time **25 minutes (plus an hour to marinate)**

Cooking time **6 minutes**

Smoked salmon steaks 2

For the marinade

Harissa paste 1 tbsp

Soy sauce 1 tbsp

Soft brown sugar ½ tbsp

For the mango and lime curd

Fresh mango ½, skinned

Lime 1, juice and zest

Caster sugar 100g

Butter 50g

Eggs 3, (2 whole and 1 yolk)

For the quinoa

Quinoa 100g

Lime 1, juice and zest

Fresh mango ½, skinned and cut into 1cm cubes

Fresh ginger 2.5cm piece, grated

Harissa paste 1 tbsp

Salt and pepper to season

For the salad

Courgette 1, peeled into ribbons

Rhubarb 1 stick, peeled into ribbons

Caster sugar 10g

Lime 1, juice and zest

To serve

Sesame seeds 2 tsp

Oil a dash

1. **For the marinade**: combine the harissa, soy and sugar then coat the salmon. Cover it and leave in the fridge for at least an hour.

2. **For the mango and lime curd:** blend the mango in a food processor until smooth. Add the lime juice and zest, then blend again. Transfer the mixture into a saucepan with the caster sugar and butter. Bring to the boil then reduce to a simmer, ensuring the butter has completely melted.

3. Whisk the eggs in a bowl, then add to the curd mix. Turn the heat very low and stir continuously, ensuring the texture remains smooth and doesn't curdle. Once the mix starts to thicken so that it will coat the back of a spoon, remove from the heat and allow to cool.

4. **For the quinoa:** rinse the quinoa under cold water, then place in a pan with 200g water and bring to the boil. Reduce the heat to a simmer and cook for 10-15 minutes or until tender. Run under cold water to stop the cooking process, then drain and transfer to a bowl.

5. Add the lime juice and zest, mango, ginger and harissa to the quinoa. Mix, season and set aside.

6. **For the salad:** mix the courgette and rhubarb ribbons, then add caster sugar (enough to take the sharpness from the rhubarb) and lime juice and zest.

7. **To serve:** preheat the oven to 180°c / gas 4. Heat an ovenproof, non-stick frying pan and add oil. Carefully place the salmon skin-side down for 2 minutes, before turning and transferring to the oven for 3-4 minutes.

8. Place a generous spoonful of quinoa, along with a handful of the salad in the centre of each plate. Put a salmon steak on top and drizzle with the curd. Finish with a sprinkle of sesame seeds and a drizzle of oil.

BLOCK

Barnstaple, Devon

Barnstaple's hip hangout serves up coffee to complement the quality of its eclectic, global food and Northern Soul tunes.

Andy and Tran Stephenson gave up corporate life in 2017 to create their dream cafe, and found a home among the quirky band of indies on historic Butchers Row.

Visit for well-crafted coffee from Bristol roastery Clifton (served in retro 70s stoneware) alongside bowls of steaming pho and creative homemade bakes such as carrot and white chocolate shortbread.

Recipe
CHICKEN SHAWARMA

CHICKEN SHAWARMA

Recipe by Andy Stephenson of Block

Serves **4**

Preparation time **30 minutes (plus overnight marinating time)**

Cooking time **15 minutes**

For the marinade

Lemon 1, juice

Garlic 6 cloves, finely grated

Red onion 1, finely grated

Ground black pepper 2 tsp

Ground cumin 2 tsp

Paprika 2 tsp

Turmeric 1 tsp

Crushed chilli flakes 1 tsp

Cinnamon ½ tsp

Good quality olive oil 200ml

Free-range chicken thighs 8, skinned and boned

For the garlic yogurt

Greek yogurt 300ml

Garlic clove 1, finely grated

Coarse salt and crushed black pepper to season

Flatbreads 4

Mixed salad leaves

Plum tomatoes 2, sliced into wedges

Cucumber ½, sliced

Red onion ½, finely sliced

Pickled red cabbage

Pomegranate ½, seeds

Za'atar 4 tbsp

1. *For the marinade:* the day before serving, mix all of the ingredients into a paste and thickly coat the chicken thighs. If the paste doesn't stick, add more oil. Cover and leave in the fridge overnight.

2. *For the garlic yogurt:* mix the ingredients in a bowl. If it's too thick, loosen with a splash of milk.

3. Grill or barbecue the chicken thighs in a little oil for around 4 minutes on each side until cooked through. Set aside to rest for a few minutes. Warm the flatbreads in the oven or on the barbecue.

4. *To assemble:* put a warmed flatbread on a plate, layer with the mixed leaves, tomato, cucumber, onion and cabbage.

5. Slice the cooked chicken into strips and add to the flatbreads with a handful of pomegranate seeds and a sprinkle of za'atar. Finish with a drizzle of garlic yogurt dressing.

6. *To fold:* fold the bottom third of the flatbread up, fold in the right side and then bring the left side over the top and secure with a short wooden skewer.

DRINK PAIRING

Iced Chai Latte

PLAYLIST PAIRING

Earthquake

Bobbi Lynn

'Coat chickpeas in the **shawarma** spice mix to make a *veggie version*'

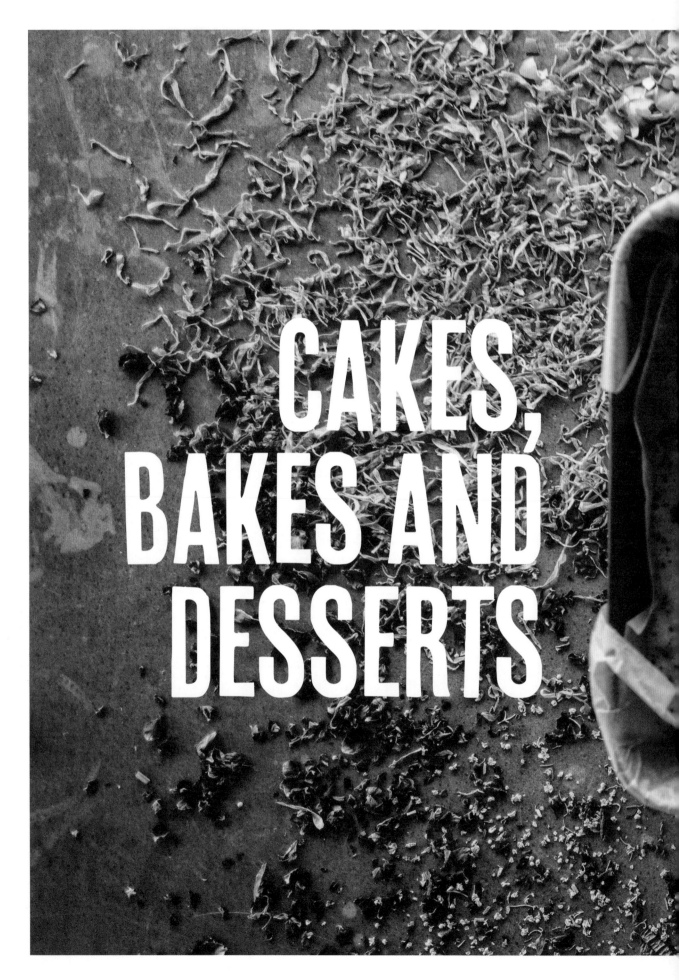

CAKES, BAKES AND DESSERTS

CAMERINO BAKERY

Dublin, Republic of Ireland

One of the *Irish Independent*'s '*30 things to do in Dublin before you die*', this indie bakery, cakery and coffee shop is definitely one for the bucket list.

The media mentions haven't stopped rolling in since owner Caryna Camerino opened the tiny space on Capel Street in 2014. It's garnered some gongs too: the raspberry chocolate cheesecake brownie won gold at the Blas na hÉireann Irish Food Awards, while its peanut butter brother scooped bronze.

Recipe
CITRUS POUND CAKE

CITRUS POUND CAKE

Recipe by Caryna Camerino of Camerino Bakery

Serves **6**

Preparation time **20 minutes**

Cooking time **45 minutes**

Ruby grapefruit 1
Orange 1
Lemon 1
Free-range eggs 2
Granulated sugar 220g
Irish salted
butter 150g, softened
Greek yogurt 140g
Vanilla extract 1 tsp
Self-raising flour 225g
Icing sugar to decorate

1. Preheat the oven to 160°c / gas 3 and line a medium loaf tin with baking parchment.

2. Reserving a couple of thin slices of each of the fruits, finely zest the remainder of the skins into a large bowl.

3. Add the eggs, sugar, butter, yogurt and vanilla extract to the bowl, then beat until combined.

4. Sift in the flour and mix until smooth.

5. Pour the batter into the lined loaf tin and bake for 45 minutes or until golden and a skewer comes out clean.

6. Once cooked, remove from the oven and allow to cool for 20 minutes. Then remove from the tin and let the cake cool completely.

7. Before serving, dress the loaf with the fruit slices and dust with icing sugar.

The yogurt helps bring out the bright tang of the citrus'

COFFEE PAIRING

Roasted Brown
Ethiopian Chelelektu

Filter

PLAYLIST PAIRING

Friday I'm In Love
Yo La Tengo

LAY OF THE LAND

Settle, North Yorkshire

This is a one-stop shop for foliage, fodder and fantastic coffee. Hidden away among leafy plants and luscious pots in the heart of a bonsai-sized garden centre, you'll stumble upon a light, bright, contemporary coffee shop with an oak-sized reputation.

Chef James Lay trained at Michelin starred Northcote in Langho, and his menus at Lay of the Land have foodies and gardeners alike raving about the homemade pork pies, scotch eggs and sweet potato falafel.

Recipe
COFFEE DOUGHNUTS

COFFEE DOUGHNUTS

Recipe by James Lay of Lay of the Land

Serves **12**

Preparation time **20 minutes (plus 2 hours proving)**

Cooking time **20 minutes**

For the doughnuts

Water 120ml

Dried yeast 14g

Plain flour 365g

Strong white flour 265g

Caster sugar 90g

Salt 12g

Free-range egg yolks 6, large

Ground cardamom ½ tsp

Ground cinnamon ½ tsp

Unsalted butter 70g, softened

For the custard

Whole milk 250ml

Double cream 50ml

Vanilla pod ½,
split lengthways

Free-range egg yolks 4, large

Caster sugar 60g

Cornflour 15g

Plain flour 15g

Espresso 2 shots

1. *For the doughnuts:* put the water, 7g of yeast and 100g of plain flour into a large bowl and beat for 6 minutes. Cover with clingfilm and leave in a warm place for 45 minutes.

2. Add the remaining plain flour and yeast, strong white flour, caster sugar, salt, egg yolks, cardamom and cinnamon to the bowl and mix for a further 10 minutes. Slowly beat in the butter for around 5 minutes. Cover and set aside for 45 minutes.

3. Portion the dough into 12 equal pieces and roll into balls with the palms of your hands. Place on a floured surface and slightly flatten, cover with a damp tea towel and allow to prove for a further 45 minutes.

4. Heat a deep fat fryer to 160°c. Fry the doughnuts for 3-4 minutes on each side until golden. Remove, drain on kitchen paper, roll in caster sugar and allow to cool.

5. *For the custard:* bring the milk, cream and vanilla to the boil over a medium heat.

6. In another bowl, whisk together the eggs and sugar, then add the cornflour and flour. Slowly stir the milk mixture into this, then add the espresso.

7. Return the mix to the pan and heat until it begins to thicken. Remove from the heat and allow to cool.

8. *To assemble:* once everything is cold, whisk the custard and transfer to a piping bag. Make a small cut in the side of each doughnut and fill with custard.

COFFEE PAIRING

Casa Espresso

Espresso

PLAYLIST PAIRING

*Wake Me Up Before
You Go-Go*

Wham!

'If you don't have a fryer, use a deep pan of oil'

ESTABLISHED COFFEE

Belfast, Northern Ireland

However much you don't want to be 'that guy', impeccably prepared coffee and perfectly presented brunch plates make Instagramming your Established experience inevitable.

Owners Bridgeen Barbour and Mark Ashridge have been crafting exceptional coffee here since 2013, earning the contemporary cafe a reputation as one of the best in Belfast – so you won't be the only one waving your phone in the air.

Recipe
CHURRO-WAFFLE ICE CREAM SANDWICH

'If you've got the time, serve with homemade ice cream and *peanut brittle*'

COFFEE PAIRING

3FE Kiamaina

AeroPress

PLAYLIST PAIRING

Sexual Healing

Hot 8 Brass Band

CHURRO-WAFFLE AND COOKIE DOUGH ICE CREAM SANDWICH

Recipe by Phillip, Jane, Stephen and Michael of Established Coffee

Serves **4**

Preparation time **25 minutes**

Cooking time **20 minutes**

For the waffle
Unsalted butter 70g
Dark brown sugar 45g
Vanilla extract 5g
Salt 4g
Ground cinnamon 2g
Ground cardamom 2g
Plain flour 125g
Free-range egg 1, large
Baking soda 1g

For the cookie dough
Caster sugar 85g
Dark brown sugar 170g
Butter 80g, softened
Free-range egg 1, large
Vanilla extract ½ tsp
Organic plain flour 250g
Baking soda 2.5g
Maldon Sea Salt 2.5g
Chocolate chips 120g

To serve
Ice cream
Peanut brittle
Chocolate ganache

Equipment
Waffle iron

1. *For the waffle:* put the butter, sugar, vanilla, salt, cinnamon and cardamom in a pan with 235ml of water and bring to a simmer over a medium heat. Add the flour and stir with a wooden spoon until the mixture forms a thick dough.

2. Keep cooking and stirring for another minute until a thin film forms on the sides of the pan. Remove from the heat and continue to stir for a further minute. Allow to cool.

3. Preheat a waffle iron to a medium-high heat.

4. Beat the egg into the cooled dough with a whisk until smooth. Add the baking powder and beat again.

5. Pour 2-3 tbsp of the waffle dough in the centre of the griddle, close and cook for 6-7 minutes until brown and crispy. When cooked, cool the waffle on a rack for 5-10 minutes then brush with melted butter and sprinkle with sugar.

6. *For the cookie dough:* beat the sugars and butter together until pale, then fold in the egg and vanilla.

7. Sift the flour, baking soda and salt together. Combine with the wet ingredients until fully incorporated and then add the chocolate chips.

8. Once mixed, place the dough on clingfilm and roll into a log 5-7cm in diameter and leave to set in the fridge before slicing into rounds when needed.

9. *To serve:* layer the waffle with a disk of the cookie dough, ice cream, peanut brittle and warm chocolate ganache.

MORE SEATING
UPSTAIRS

BAKESMITHS

Bristol, South West

Seasoned cafe clientele will have encountered Cakesmiths' colourful compilations of tempting traybakes and wickedly gooey brownies at coffee houses across the UK. But to experience its doughy delights hot from the oven, a pilgrimage to the Bristol HQ, Bakesmiths, is in order.

Churning out chewy sourdough loaves, chocolate-laced banana bread and sweet masterpieces that would make Prue Leith proud, this contemporary bakery on the corner of Whiteladies Road is a cathedral to coffee and carbs.

Recipe
ENGLISH GARDEN CAKE

...DEN CAKE

...iart (chief cake inventor) of Bakesmiths

...ion time **40 minutes**

...ing time **1 hour 10 minutes**

For the cake
Caster sugar 260g

Lemon 1, zest, finely grated

Free-range eggs 3, large

Virgin rapeseed oil 225ml

Vanilla extract 1 tsp

Cucumber 60g, grated and
seeds removed

Courgette 160g, grated

Fresh mint leaves 12g,
finely chopped

Plain flour 280g, sifted

Baking powder 12g

Salt 3g

For the frosting
Salted butter 35g, softened

Cream cheese 70g

Elderflower cordial 25g

Icing sugar 310g, sifted

Edible dried flowers to decorate

1. Preheat the oven to 150°c / gas 2.

2. **For the cake:** mix the sugar and lemon zest together with a wooden spoon. Continue until the sugar has the consistency of damp sand and smells super lemony. Add the eggs, oil and vanilla extract, then beat until smooth. Mix in the cucumber, courgette and mint.

3. Gently add the flour, baking powder and salt, then fold in until fully combined. The mixture should be quite runny so don't worry if it seems wet. Pour the batter into a lined square baking tin and gently level out. Bake in the oven for 60-70 minutes, or until a skewer comes out clean. Allow to fully cool.

4. **For the frosting:** mix the butter with the cream cheese and beat until smooth with no lumps. Add the elderflower cordial and beat until combined, then gently mix in the icing sugar. Once combined, beat until thick and pale.

5. **To assemble:** spread the frosting over the surface of the cake with a small palette knife. Sprinkle with whatever petals take your fancy – rose, marigold, cornflower, elderflower and hibiscus all work well. Pop it in the fridge for 20 minutes for the frosting to set before cutting and serving.

COFFEE PAIRING

*Clifton Coffee
Daterra Monte Cristo*

Americano

PLAYLIST PAIRING

Terraform

Novo Amor & Ed Tullett

'If cucumber isn't your thing, swap for apple instead'

THE LOFT CAFE & BAKERY

Haddington, East Lothian

A light and bright top floor of an 18th century stone building is home to the appropriately named Loft Cafe.

Local provenance and seasonality are at the heart of this popular foodie destination where greedy delights are served from breakfast onwards.

Regulars know to plump for the house specials – all hand crafted by the team in the kitchen – which includes beef stovies with oatcakes and chutney.

Recipe
VEGAN BANANA BREAD

VEGAN BANANA BREAD

Recipe by Anita Leveridge of The Loft Cafe & Bakery

Serves **8**

Preparation time **20 minutes**

Cooking time **45 minutes–1 hour**

Ripe bananas 4, peeled
Sunflower oil 6 tbsp
Maple syrup 3 tbsp
Vanilla extract 1 tsp
Mixed spice 2 tsp
Ground almonds 120g
Self-raising flour 200g
Baking powder 1 tsp
Salt a pinch
Prunes 10, roughly chopped
Dried apricots 10,
roughly chopped
Pistachios 100g

1. Preheat the oven to 160°c / gas 3 and line a medium loaf tin with parchment paper.

2. In a bowl, mash the bananas with a fork and then add the oil, maple syrup and vanilla extract. Combine.

3. Add the mixed spice, ground almonds, flour, baking powder and salt to the wet mixture. Gently combine with a wooden spoon.

4. Carefully stir the prunes, apricots and pistachios into the mix.

5. Pour into the prepared loaf tin and bake for 45 minutes, or until a skewer comes out clean.

6. Allow to cool for 10 minutes before turning out onto a wire rack to cool completely.

'Swap in dried fruit and nuts to taste – pecans also work really well'

COFFEE PAIRING

Artisan Roast Janszoon
Oat Milk Noisette

PLAYLIST PAIRING

Better Together
Callaghan

STRONG ADOLFOS

Wadebridge, Cornwall

Surf, cycle and coffee cultures collide at this roadside hangout where bikers pull up on vintage choppers, colourful boards adorn the walls and baristas craft Cornish espresso.

The unlikely spot on the A39 near Wadebridge doesn't simply draw in surfers fresh from the waves and coffee fans travelling through the county. A killer kitchen team creates brunch, lunch and epic Scandi bakes from scratch, so Strong Adolfos has also become a favourite with holidaymakers and locals willing to make a short detour for Swedish delights which include cardamom buns and drömmar cookies.

Recipe
CARROT AND PARSNIP CAKE

'Use **carrots or parsnips** depending on what you've got - just make sure they weigh 450g in total'

SWEDISH CARROT AND PARSNI[P]
LIME CREAM CHEESE FROSTING

Recipe by Mathilda Fristrom Eldridge of Strong Adolfos

Serves **10**

Preparation time **30 minutes**

Cooking time **35-40 minutes**

For the cake

Free-range eggs 4

Caster sugar 250g

Plain flour 300g

Bicarbonate of soda 3 tsp

Ground cinnamon 1½ tsp

Ground cardamom 1½ tsp

Carrots 225g, peeled and grated

Parsnips 225g, peeled and grated

Vanilla bean paste 1 tsp

Sunflower oil 220ml

For the frosting

Icing sugar 400g

Butter 80g, softened

Cream cheese 150g

Lime 1, zest

Vanilla bean paste ½ tsp

Lime wedges to decorate

Blueberries to decorate

Rosemary sprigs to decorate

1. Preheat the oven to 170°c / gas 3.

2. **For the cake:** grease and line a 25cm round baking tin with baking parchment.

3. Whisk the eggs and sugar in a mixer on high speed until pale and fluffy. Then sieve in the flour, bicarbonate of soda, cinnamon and cardamom and fold until combined.

4. Add the carrots, parsnips, vanilla bean paste and oil and fold until combined.

5. Pour the mixture into the prepared cake tin and level.

6. Bake for 35-40 minutes or until a skewer comes out clean. Leave to cool completely while you make the frosting.

7. **For the frosting:** sieve the icing sugar into a large bowl then add all of the other ingredients and whisk on a high speed until smooth and fluffy.

8. **To assemble:** cover the top of the cake with the frosting then decorate with lime wedges, blueberries and rosemary sprigs.

COFFEE PAIRING

Origin Coffee Roasters

Black Filter

PLAYLIST PAIRING

Solitude Is Bliss

Tame Impala

FINCA

Dorchester, Dorset

Dorchester's original speciality coffee shop, Finca is an excellent find for own-roasted, top-notch coffee served in a relaxed environment which is all wood and cheer.

In summer, the bi-fold windows open to let the sun in, and local caffeine fiends make a beeline for the outdoor seating, seasonally-changing nitro cold brew and their pick of the counter which heaves with homemade cakes and sourdough.

Recipe
FRUIT AND NUT CHOCOLATE SLICE

FRUIT AND NUT CHOCOLATE SLICE

...t of Finca

...on time **20 minutes**

...ng time **2 hours to set in fridge**

Ground almonds 200g

Dates 400g, chopped

Cacao powder 25g

Chia seeds 50g

Coconut oil 60g, softened

Raspberry jam 180g

Mixed nuts 100g,
finely chopped

Dried cranberries and
raisins 150g

Dark chocolate 400g

Smooth peanut butter 180g

♪

PLAYLIST PAIRING

All We Do

Oh Wonder

COFFEE PAIRING

Finca Altos de Erapuca

Espresso

1. Blitz the almonds and dates in a blender for around a minute until combined.

2. Add the cacao and chia seeds and blend for 20 seconds. Next, add the coconut oil and blend for a further 30 seconds.

3. Turn out the blended ingredients into a bowl, add 2-3 tbsp of water and gently combine with a fork until they start to clump together. Don't add too much water as the mixture will become too wet.

4. Line a 20cm baking tin with greaseproof paper. Spoon the mixture in and use a fork to spread the ingredients evenly around the tin. Place a second piece of greaseproof paper on top and use a second baking tin to gently press down and evenly distribute the mix. Remove the top tin and paper. Spread the jam evenly on top of the mix.

5. Place the chopped nuts in a bowl with the dried fruit, combine and then sprinkle evenly on top of the jam layer. Use a fork to distribute the fruit and nut mix. Again, use the second tin and greaseproof paper to ensure everything is flat.

6. In a saucepan, melt the chocolate on a low-medium heat, stirring frequently to ensure it doesn't burn. Once the chocolate has melted, add the peanut butter and stir on a low heat until the two combine.

7. Pour the chocolate mix on top of the ingredients already in the baking tin. Use the back of a spoon to quickly push the chocolate mix to the edges and corners of the tin – be careful not to dislodge the mix already in the tin. Bang the tin on the worktop for an even finish.

8. Place the tin in the fridge for a couple of hours or, even better, overnight. Remove the fruit and nut bar from the tin and, using a warm knife, cut into 12 slices.

'This dairy- and gluten-free slice is chilled in the fridge so **no baking** is required'

THE CEILIDH PLACE

Ullapool, Scotland

Overlooking Loch Broom and the Dearg hills beyond, The Ceilidh Place is nestled in a perfect corner of Wester Ross.

Inside, you'll find plenty of perfect corners to relax in, whether you're reading a book from the bookshop, admiring the varied exhibitions from visiting and local artists, or just enjoying a great cup of coffee and one of these fabulous scones. Hang out long enough and you might just catch a gig from the diverse programme of events which runs all year.

'Celebrating all the arts, from visual to culinary, we're at the end of the A835 and the centre of the universe,' say the team at The Ceilidh Place.

Recipe
FRUIT SCONES

FRUIT SCONES

Recipe by The Ceilidh Place

Makes **8**

Preparation time **15 minutes**

Cooking time **20 minutes**

Plain flour 500g

Baking powder 25g

Butter 125g,
medium-hard, cubed

Caster sugar 75g

Sultanas 75g

Free-range eggs 2

Whole milk 125ml

1. Preheat the oven to 180°c / gas 4.

2. In a large bowl, sieve together the flour
   and baking powder.

3. Rub the butter into the flour mix until combined.

4. In a separate bowl, toss together the caster sugar
   and the sultanas. Combine with the flour mixture.

5. In another bowl, whisk together the eggs and
   milk. Fold into the flour and fruit mix until the
   consistency is firm but not sticky.

6. Gently roll out the dough until it is 2.5cm
   thick and press out into 7cm rounds using
   a pastry cutter.

7. Place on a lined baking tray and cook for 20
   minutes, rotating after 15 minutes to ensure an
   even golden colour.

COFFEE PAIRING

*Glen Lyon Red Stag
Seasonal Espresso*

Flat White

PLAYLIST PAIRING

Summer

Elephant Sessions

'Coating the sultanas in sugar gives them a slightly *chispy caramelisation*'

STAR ANISE CAFE

Stroud, Gloucestershire

With a lively schedule of music, poetry, theatre and storytelling events keeping the gorgeous grub and quality coffee company, a trip to community conscious Star Anise provides nourishment for both mind and body.

For appetites in need of satiating, there's a wholefood menu stuffed full of fish, veggie and vegan fodder, while caffeinated comfort comes courtesy of Bristol's Extract which stocks the cafe with its Original Espresso Blend.

Recipe
AVOCADO CHOCOLATE TORTE

CHOCOLATE AVOCADO TORTE

Recipe by Nicholas Allan of Star Anise Cafe

Serves **8-10**

Preparation time **20-25 minutes**

For the base

Dates 100g, pre-soaked

Porridge oats 150g, toasted

Nuts (not peanuts) 200g, toasted

Sunflower seeds 50g, toasted

Cacao powder 40g

Rapadura (unrefined whole cane sugar) 70g

Salt a pinch

Rice syrup (alternatively, use maple or honey) 35ml

Coconut oil 70g

For the filling

Dark chocolate 150g

Rice syrup 150ml

Coconut oil 150g

Ripe avocados 2 large, peeled and destoned

Cacao powder 75g

Vanilla extract 1 tsp

Salt a pinch

1. **For the base:** place all of the dry ingredients in a food processor and blitz. Add the syrup and coconut oil and blitz again to combine.

2. Lightly brush the bottom of a metal spring-form tin with oil. Pour the base mixture into the tin and firmly press it down with the back of a spoon until compact and level.

3. **For the filling:** melt the chocolate in a bowl over simmering water. Once melted, add the syrup and coconut oil.

4. Pour the mixture into a food processor, add the avocado, cacao, vanilla and salt and blitz until smooth and glistening. If it doesn't have a shiny texture, add a dash more of the syrup.

5. **To assemble:** pour the filling onto the base and allow to set at room temperature. Decorate with flaked almonds and shaved dark chocolate.

'Use a **vegan** variety of choc to make the torte totally plant-based'

COFFEE PAIRING

Extract Coffee Roasters Original Espresso

Espresso

PLAYLIST PAIRING

Cumbia del Olvido

Nicola Cruz

URBUN CAFE

Dublin, Republic of Ireland

A mission to serve amazing food and awesome coffee under one industrial roof is what inspired Katie Gilroy to launch Urbun Cafe in the Dublin suburb of Cabinteely.

Katie started out selling cakes at a local farmers' market, where she stumbled upon the smoothest, sweetest coffee she'd ever tasted. The result? Setting up her own speciality cafe.

Seven years later and Badger & Dodo beans still feature as the house blend, as well as providing the weekly-changing single origin.

Recipe
VEGAN OAT 'N' NUT BARS

VEGAN OAT 'N' NUT BARS

Recipe by Katie Gilroy of Urbun Cafe

Serves **12**

Preparation time **10 minutes**

Cooking time **15 minutes**

Dates 400g

Extra virgin coconut oil 3 tbsp

Oats 500g

Raisins 100g

Sunflower seeds 50g

Pumpkin seeds 50g

Desiccated coconut 25g

Goji berries (or
cranberries) 25g

1. Preheat the oven to 165°c / gas 3. Line a rectangular tin with baking parchment.

2. Put the dates in a pan and cover with water. Bring to the boil and allow to steep for 10 minutes before removing from the heat and blitzing into a paste.

3. In a bowl, mix the paste with the rest of the ingredients until combined.

4. Press the mixture into the prepared baking tin and apply pressure to ensure the bars are even.

5. Bake for around 15 minutes until golden.

6. Allow to cool and then slice into 12 pieces.

Throw in a hanful of 70 per cent cocoa chips for a chocolate hit

DRINK PAIRING

Spiced Chai Latte

PLAYLIST PAIRING

Keep Your Name

Dirty Projectors

ATKINSONS THE BAKERY

Lancaster, Lancashire

Despite the parade of syphons bubbling away at the bar and the rare beans celebrated on the chalkboard menu, Atkinsons' beautiful home at The Hall attracts coffee folk with all levels of knowledge.

The whole set-up in this gorgeous old parish hall is pleasingly homemade: the beans are roasted next door at Atkinsons' eco roastery while the house bakery crafts decadent cakes which provide a perfect pairing for the beautiful brews.

Recipe
RHUBARB, LIME AND COCONUT CAKE

RHUBARB, LIME AND COCONUT CAKE

Recipe by Debbie Kaye of Atkinsons The Bakery

Serves **7**

Preparation time **20 minutes**

Cooking time **55-60 minutes**

For the cake

Butter 150g

Caster sugar 170g

Free-range eggs 3

Plain flour 105g

Baking powder ¾ tsp

Desiccated coconut 100g

Rhubarb 250g, chopped

For the lemon and lime drizzle

Lemon 1, zest and juice

Lime 1, zest and juice

Water 60ml

Caster sugar 115g

Cream cheese
topping to decorate

Seasonal fruit to decorate

1. Preheat the oven to 180°c / gas 4. Line a medium loaf tin with parchment paper.

2. **For the cake:** in a large bowl, beat together the butter and sugar until light and creamy.

3. Add the eggs one at a time, beating well between each addition.

4. Sift the flour and baking powder together and gently fold into the egg mixture with the coconut and rhubarb.

5. Pour the mixture into the prepared loaf tin and bake for 55 minutes to an hour, or until a skewer comes out clean. Allow to cool in the tin then turn out onto a wire rack.

6. **For the lemon and lime drizzle:** place all of the ingredients in a pan and bring to the boil. Simmer until the sugar dissolves and the mixture becomes thick and syrupy. Drizzle the syrup over the cake.

7. Decorate the cake with a cream cheese topping and seasonal fruits.

Try topping the cake with sliced nectarines pistachios and pomegranate seeds

COFFEE PAIRING

*Atkinsons Coffee Roasters
Ethiopian Hambella Natural*

Syphon

PLAYLIST PAIRING

Coconut

Harry Nilsson

DARK WOODS COFFEE

Marsden, West Yorkshire

2018 was a busy year for the growing team at Dark Woods Coffee in Marsden. The Huddersfield roastery added ten Great Taste gongs to its sizable silverware collection, as well as securing the privilege of roasting for Liberty of London's new food hall.

Supplying speciality coffee shops across the country, all of Dark Woods' prize-winning blends, exclusive micro lots and seasonal single origins are roasted at its renovated textile mill on the banks of the River Colne.

Recipe
MALTED CHOCOLATE MOUSSE
WITH CASCARA COLD BREW MARTINI

...OLATE MOUSSE WITH
...OLD BREW MARTINI

...Meikle-Janney of Dark Woods Coffee

...ration time **20 minutes (cold brew and cascara syrup day before)**

For the cold brew

Panama natural
coffee 60g, ground

Water 1l

For the cascara syrup

Cascara 20g

Water 200ml

Sugar 200g

For the mousse

Thick double cream 300ml

Horlicks powder 50g

Coffee grounds a pinch
(optional)

Chocolate 300g, mix of dark
and milk, melted

For each martini

Cold brew 50ml

Vodka 25ml

Cascara syrup 25ml

Ice

Maraschino cherry to garnish

1. **For the cold brew:** steep the coffee grounds in the water overnight. Filter it the following morning. Chill in the fridge.

2. **For the cascara syrup:** in a pan, brew the cascara in the water. Strain the cascara using a fine sieve and add the sugar to the liquid. Simmer the liquid until the sugar has melted. Bottle then chill.

3. **For the mousse:** gently whip the cream until peaks begin to form, being cautious not to overwhip. Fold in the Horlicks and coffee grounds.

4. Gently fold the melted chocolate into the cream mixture. Spoon the mousse into espresso cups and refrigerate for at least an hour before serving.

5. **To assemble the martini:** pour the cold brew, vodka and cascara into a cocktail shaker with ice and shake. Strain into a martini glass and garnish with a maraschino cherry.

♫

PLAYLIST PAIRING

Love Is The Message
Yussef Dayes & Alfa Mist

'We use our *Great Taste Award* winning *Panama coffee* for its sweet cherry notes'

COCKTAILS AND DRINKS

NORTH STAR COFFEE ROASTERS

Leeds, West Yorkshire

Establishing North Star in 2013, Alex and Holly Kragiopoulos were the first roasters in Leeds to bronze beans of the highest grade and work with speciality-focused arabica farmers.

The team continue to strive to roast the best coffee they can get their hands on, sourcing in a way that puts the producer first and ensures their farming is profitable. You can watch the roasting magic in action – and road test this coffee-infused G&T – at the Leeds Dock roastery, cafe and training space.

Recipe
C, G&T

G&T

Recipe by Holly Kragiopoulos of North Star Coffee Roasters

Serves **1**

Preparation time **2 minutes (filter coffee 1 hour in advance)**

Filter coffee 75ml, cold
Harewood Gin 25ml
Orange juice a splash
Ice to serve
Quality tonic water 75ml
Orange peel a twist

1. Brew the filter coffee using a pourover method such as V60 or Clever Dripper, or via an automated filter machine. Allow to cool.

2. Pour the gin, orange juice and coffee into a tall glass and stir.

3. Add a few ice cubes and top with tonic water. Garnish with an orange twist and serve.

Pick a lightly roasted, fruity coffee. We use a single origin Burundi

FOOD PAIRING

*Clementine, feta and
chicory salad*

PLAYLIST PAIRING

Porcelain

Moby

EXTRACT COFFEE ROASTERS

Bristol, South West

Roasting in Bristol since 2007, Extract are one of the South West's coffee pioneers. The speciality set-up has come a long way since its coffee cart origins selling beans on College Green. The growing team now roast a globetrotting array of coffees for specialist cafes across the country from their Gatton Road roastery and continue to thrive through innovation.

Recipe
DISCO FUNK NEGRONI

DISCO FUNK NEGRONI

Recipe by James Catton of Extract Coffee Roasters

Serves **1**

Preparation time **10 minutes**

Discarded Sweet Cascara
Vermouth 25ml

Psychopomp Wõden Gin 25ml

Extract Original
Espresso 60ml

Honey 15g

Orange peel

Ice cubes

Orange twist to garnish

1. Pour the vermouth and gin into a mixing glass with ice and spin for 30 seconds.

2. Pull 2 shots (60ml) of espresso. Add the honey to the hot coffee and stir.

3. Add the coffee and honey mixture to the mixing glass and spin for 30 seconds.

4. Using a match or lighter, flame the orange peel over the drink.

5. Put a couple of large ice cubes in a tumbler and strain the drink into the glass. Garnish with a twist of orange.

'Discarded make vermouth from single origin Guatemalan cascara'

FOOD PAIRING

Hot chocolate fudge cake

PLAYLIST PAIRING

Hit It And Quit It
Funkadelic

ARTEMIS

Womersley, North Yorkshire

Stocked at over 50 indies across the country, Artemis' cold brew has made waves since founder Ben Barker launched the product in 2015.

With an emphasis on sustainability and traceability, Ben and his team of coffee alchemists source the highest quality beans to craft their two-time Great Taste award winning drink, as well as a luxe coffee concentrate.

Recipe
ESPRESSO MARTIKI

ESPRESSO MARTIKI

Recipe by Ben Barker at Artemis

Serves **1**

Preparation time **2 minutes**

Bacardi 8yo rum 30ml

Artemis Coffee
Concentrate 30ml

Almond syrup 5ml

Pineapple juice 20ml

Ice cubes

Edible flowers to garnish

1. Chill a coupe glass in the freezer.

2. Pour the rum, coffee concentrate, almond syrup and pineapple juice into a cocktail shaker with ice. Shake well.

3. Fine strain the mix into the chilled glass, garnish with edible flowers and serve.

'Chill a coupe or martini glass in advance for the perfect serve'

FOOD PAIRING

*Pineapple and almond
upside-down cake*

PLAYLIST PAIRING

Africa

Toto

DEAR GREEN COFFEE ROASTERS

Glasgow, Scotland

Founded in 2011 by Lisa Lawson, Dear Green has been instrumental in driving speciality coffee in Scotland. Passionate about the whole coffee process, the Glasgow roastery has always been steered by its ethical and social conscience.

Beans generally come from South America and Africa, though the key to sourcing everything is *'quality flavour notes and seasonality,'* says Lisa.

Recipe
THE COFFEE CHERRY

COFFEE CHERRY

Recipe by Daniel Ormonde of Dear Green Coffee Roasters

Serves **4**

Preparation time **2 minutes (tea 24 hours in advance)**

Cherry tea 6g, brewed in 200ml cold water in the fridge for 24 hours

Gin (or non-alcoholic alternative) 100ml

Clear honey 20g

Ice 180g

Espresso 90ml

Aromatic tonic water 60ml

Orange zest to serve

1. Chill four glasses in the freezer until cold and misted.

2. Strain the cold brew tea into a jug.

3. Add the gin, honey and 100g of ice to the tea in the jug and stir well. Set aside.

4. Remove the glasses from the freezer, put 20g of ice in each one, and then pull two double shots of espresso over each (Daniel uses two long shots of Colombia San Antonio from Tolima, a medium roast, brewed to an espresso recipe of 19/34/45).

5. Strain the ice from the tea mixture, then pour 75ml of the tea mixture into each glass.

6. Top each drink with 15ml of aromatic tonic water.

7. Garnish with a twist of orange zest and serve.

'Cold brewing the tea achieves vibrant cherry notes without too much sweetness'

FOOD PAIRING

Brazilian orange cake

PLAYLIST PAIRING

Border Girl

Young Fathers

COALTOWN ROASTERY CANTEEN

Ammanford, South Wales

Coaltown's brand spanking new HQ on the outskirts of Ammanford is shaking up the coffee scene in South Wales.

The huge space - furnished with house plants, retired school chairs and beautifully designed machinery - on the outskirts of the ex-mining town is a melting pot of coffee culture. An espresso bar, canteen, training school and roastery all co-exist under one roof.

Recipe
ICED JAPANESE MARMALADE POUROVER

ICED JAPANESE MARMALADE POUROVER

Recipe by Bronwen Tinney of Coaltown Roastery Canteen

Serves **2**

Preparation time **10 minutes**

Ice cubes 200g

Marmalade 5 tsp

Coffee 40g, ground to
filter consistency

Water 300ml

Tangerines 3, chopped

Equipment

Chemex

Filter paper

1. Put the ice cubes and marmalade in the base of the Chemex.

2. Place the paper filter in the funnel of the Chemex and add the ground coffee.

3. Slowly pour the heated water over for 3-4 minutes.

4. Remove the paper filter and add the tangerines to the Chemex.

5. Gently swirl the contents of the Chemex and serve over more ice.

'This looks gorgeous served in a glass with ice and a tangerine slice'

FOOD PAIRING

Clementine polenta cake

PLAYLIST PAIRING

Australia Street

Sticky Fingers

THE PLAYLIST

Each cafe and roastery has paired their dish with the perfect track. Here's the playlist in its entirety

You can also find it on Spotify:

search for INDY CAFE COOKBOOK

Track	Artist
Highway To Hell	AC/DC
'Til It's Over	Anderson Paak
On A Rooftop	Anna Mieke
Glitter & Gold	Barns Courtney
Earthquake	Bobbi Lynn
Better Together	Callaghan
Stare Too Long	Corrosion Of Conformity
Move On Up	Curtis Mayfield
Captain Brunch	Czarface & MF Doom
SoWhat	Dil Withers
Keep Your Name	Dirty Projectors
Summer	Elephant Sessions
Let's Do It, Let's Fall In Love	Ella Fitzgerald
Hit It And Quit It	Funkadelic
Shotgun	George Ezra
Coconut	Harry Nilsson
Sexual Healing	Hot 8 Brass Band
Waiting On The World To Change	John Mayer
Ephrata	Joshua Burnside
Heavy, California	Jungle
Con Todo El Mundo	Khruangbin
Porcelain	Moby
I Need Never Get Old	Nathaniel Rateliff & The Night Sweats
Cumbia del Olvido	Nicola Cruz
Terraform	Novo Amor & Ed Tullett
All We Do	Oh Wonder
Everyday People	Sly & The Family Stone
Australia Street	Sticky Fingers
Solitude Is Bliss	Tame Impala
I'll Still Destroy You	The National
Rapper's Delight	The Sugarhill Gang
Pig	This Town Needs Guns
Africa	Toto
Into The Mystic	Van Morrison
Wake Me Up Before You Go-Go	Wham!
90 Degrees	Yazmin Lacey
Friday I'm In Love	Yo La Tengo
Border Girl	Young Fathers
Love Is The Message	Yussef Dayes & Alfa Mist

INDEX

livello B1

L'ITALIANO CON I FUMETTI

HABEMUS PAPAM

tavole: Giampiero Wallnofer

Carlo Guastalla / Ciro Massimo Naddeo

direzione editoriale: Massimo Naddeo
redazione: Carlo Guastalla, Euridice Orlandino, Chiara Sandri e Marco Dominici
progetto grafico e copertina: Lucia Cesarone
impaginazione: Gabriel de Banos
tavole: Giampiero Wallnofer

© 2013 ALMA Edizioni
Printed in Italy
ISBN: 978-88-6182-290-0
Prima edizione: marzo 2013

ALMA Edizioni
Viale dei Cadorna, 44
50129 Firenze
tel +39 055 476644
fax +39 055 473531
alma@almaedizioni.it
www.almaedizioni.it

indice

Personaggi della Storia

Alem, giornalista

Zero, vecchio amico di Alem

Effe, giornalista

Cardinale Stoppani

Cardinale Gotor

Alfonso, cuoco del Vaticano

MI CHIAMO ALEM. STRANO NOME, LO SO... HO SEMPRE AVUTO PROBLEMI PER QUESTO. MI RICORDO, QUANDO AVEVO 6 ANNI, IL MIO PRIMO GIORNO DI SCUOLA.

QUI HO QUINDICI ANNI. SONO ALLA FESTA DEL MIO MIGLIORE AMICO, ZERO. CON LUI CI CONOSCIAMO DA SEMPRE.

NO CARO, IL TUO NOME NON SI SCRIVE COSÌ... TU TI CHIAMI ALEM, NON MELA!

Mela

BUON COMPLEANNO ZERO!

AUGURI!!!

E QUESTO SONO IO A VENT'ANNI. LA RAGAZZA È EFFE, IL MIO GRANDE AMORE. CON LEI NON SONO MAI RIUSCITO A COGLIERE L'OCCASIONE GIUSTA.

STASERA? MI DISPIACE NON POSSO. DEVO STUDIARE, DOMANI HO UN ESAME IMPORTANTE. FACCIAMO DOMANI SERA?

CIAO ALEM, COME STAI? TI VA DI USCIRE CON ME STASERA?

NO, DOMANI ESCO CON PAOLO!

l'italiano con i fumetti

DOPO L'UNIVERSITÀ SONO DIVENTATO GIORNALISTA. UNA SERA, MENTRE USCIVO DAL GIORNALE, HO INCONTRATO ZERO, IL MIO VECCHIO AMICO. NON LO VEDEVO DA UN SACCO DI TEMPO. MA LUI NON MI HA NEANCHE SALUTATO, MI HA DATO UNA STRANA BUSTA E SE N'È ANDATO...

ZERO, COS'È QUESTA?

VAI IN PIAZZA SAN PIETRO, QUESTA SERA A MEZZANOTTE.

ED È COSÌ CHE È INIZIATA QUESTA ASSURDA STORIA. LA BUSTA CONTENEVA DEI DOCUMENTI SCRITTI IN UNA LINGUA CHE NON CONOSCEVO. POI C'ERA UNA LUNGA LISTA DI NOMI SCONOSCIUTI. MA LA COSA PIÙ STRANA ERA CHE OGNI PAGINA ERA PIENA DI SCRITTE E TIMBRI CHE DICEVANO TOP SECRET, SERVIZI SEGRETI, INTELLIGENCE, ECC.

NON SAPEVO COSA FARE. MI FACEVO MILLE DOMANDE. PERCHÉ ZERO MI AVEVA DATO QUEI DOCUMENTI? PERCHÉ ERA SCAPPATO? ALLA FINE SONO USCITO DALL'UFFICIO PER PORTARE TUTTO ALLA POLIZIA, MA MI SONO ACCORTO CHE QUALCUNO MI STAVA SEGUENDO. ERA UNA MACCHINA NERA, DIETRO DI ME.

UFFF ... CE L'HO FATTA!

FINALMENTE A CASA...

APPENA SONO ENTRATO HO CONTROLLATO BENE TUTTE LE STANZE: IL CORRIDOIO, LA CAMERA DA LETTO, LA CUCINA, IL SOGGIORNO E IL BAGNO. QUALCUNO POTEVA ESSERE NASCOSTO! PER FORTUNA NON C'ERA NESSUNO, LA CASA ERA SICURA.

VIA MASACCIO

MI SONO SDRAIATO SUL DIVANO E HO ASCOLTATO I MESSAGGI SULLA SEGRETERIA TELEFONICA. ERANO LE **22** E 15.

BIIP. CIAO ALEM. SONO EFFE; TI RICORDI DI ME? HO BISOGNO DI PARLARTI CON URGENZA. MA NON MI RICHIAMARE CHE PUÒ ESSERE PERICOLOSO. TI RICHIAMO IO.

22:15

EFFE... CHE STRANO... NON LA VEDO DA TANTI ANNI. COSA VUOLE ORA DA ME?

POCO DOPO SONO ANDATO IN PIZZERIA. MENTRE ORDINAVO DA MANGIARE, SI È AVVICINATO UN UOMO.

UNA MARGHERITA E UNA BIRRA.

PIAZZA SAN PIETRO, NON DIMENTICARTI.

CHI ERA QUELL'UOMO? PERCHÉ ANCHE LUI ERA SCAPPATO? C'ERA UNA SOLA COSA DA FARE: ANDARE ALL'APPUNTAMENTO IN PIAZZA SAN PIETRO. MA QUANDO SONO ARRIVATO, UN'ALTRA SORPRESA MI ASPETTAVA...

EFFE, COSA FAI QUI?

ALEM, DAMMI I DOCUMENTI!

ALL'IMPROVVISO, DI NUOVO QUELLA MACCHINA NERA. DENTRO C'ERANO DUE UOMINI. EFFE È SALTATA SULLA MIA MACCHINA MA I DUE UOMINI SONO STATI PIÙ VELOCI E HANNO SPARATO.

SONO PARTITO A TUTTA VELOCITÀ. EFFE ERA FERITA ALLA SPALLA SINISTRA.

ALEM, ANDIAMO VIA DA QUI!

BANG

EFFE, MI DEVI SPIEGARE. COS'È QUESTA STORIA? CHI SONO QUEGLI UOMINI?

NON C'È TEMPO, ORA SCAPPIAMO!

BANG

FERMATEVI!

FINE DELLA CORSA...

ZERO, QUANTO TEMPO... ERANO ANNI CHE NON CI SENTIVAMO. QUELLA MATTINA, LA MATTINA DI QUELLO STRANO SOGNO, LA SUA TELEFONATA È ARRIVATA COME UNA SORPRESA ANNUNCIATA. QUEL SOGNO COSÌ ASSURDO, O MEGLIO QUELL'INCUBO, ERA STATO COME UN'ANTICIPAZIONE, UN SEGNO DEL DESTINO.

MA QUELLO CHE MI HA DETTO MI È SEMBRATO QUASI PIÙ INCREDIBILE DEL SOGNO. ZERO INFATTI ERA DIVENTATO UNA PERSONA IMPORTANTE. ORA LAVORAVA IN VATICANO.

POICHÉ UNA SETTIMANA PRIMA IL VECCHIO PAPA ERA MORTO, ADESSO STAVA PREPARANDO IL CONCLAVE PER L'ELEZIONE DEL NUOVO PAPA. E LE SORPRESE NON ERANO FINITE LÌ...

SENTI ALEM, NOI IN TUTTI QUESTI ANNI NON CI SIAMO PIÙ VISTI, MA IO TI HO SEGUITO, HO LETTO TUTTI I TUOI ARTICOLI. SEI DIVENTATO UN BRAVO GIORNALISTA. L'HO SEMPRE DETTO CHE ERI UNA PERSONA IN GAMBA.

ADESSO IN VATICANO STANNO ARRIVANDO CARDINALI DA TUTTO IL MONDO PER IL CONCLAVE. UNO DI LORO SARÀ IL NUOVO PAPA. NOI ABBIAMO BISOGNO DI PREPARARE VELOCEMENTE LA BIOGRAFIA DEL NUOVO PAPA PER DISTRIBUIRLA ALLA STAMPA SUBITO DOPO L'ELEZIONE.

Habemus papam

LA BIOGRAFIA DEVE ESSERE PRONTA ENTRO UNA SETTIMANA DALLA FINE DEL CONCLAVE. IN QUESTA BUSTA CI SONO I DOCUMENTI CON LE INFORMAZIONI SU TUTTI I *102* CARDINALI PARTECIPANTI.

CERCHIAMO UN AUTORE GIOVANE, BRILLANTE, CAPACE DI SCRIVERE IN MODO ORIGINALE. PENSO CHE TU SIA LA PERSONA GIUSTA, PERFETTA PER QUESTO LAVORO. AH... DENTRO LA BUSTA C'È ANCHE IL CONTRATTO.

LA CIFRA PROPOSTA NEL CONTRATTO ERA MOLTO SUPERIORE AI MIEI GUADAGNI DI UN ANNO. IMPOSSIBILE DA RIFIUTARE. POI HO VISTO LA BUSTA: ERA UGUALE A QUELLA DEL MIO INCUBO! STAVO ANCORA SOGNANDO?

QUINDI ZERO HA COMINCIATO A SPIEGARMI LE REGOLE DEL CONCLAVE.

I CARDINALI RIMARRANNO CHIUSI IN UNA ZONA PROTETTA DEL VATICANO PER TUTTA LA DURATA DEL CONCLAVE E FINO A QUANDO NON AVRANNO ELETTO IL NUOVO PAPA, NESSUNO DI LORO POTRÀ USCIRE E AVERE CONTATTI CON L'ESTERNO. E NESSUNO POTRÀ ENTRARE, A PARTE POCHE PERSONE, COME ME. LE VOTAZIONI SI SVOLGERANNO NELLA CAPPELLA SISTINA, DOVE MICHELANGELO HA DIPINTO IL GIUDIZIO UNIVERSALE. QUEST'OPERA MERAVIGLIOSA DARÀ LORO L'ISPIRAZIONE.

ZERO ERA UN PERFETTO PADRONE DI CASA, PIENO DI GENTILEZZE PER IL SUO VECCHIO AMICO.

VIENI, ENTRIAMO NELLA CAPPELLA DA QUESTA PORTA SEGRETA. ORA NON C'È NESSUNO. È BELLISSIMA VERO? QUI MICHELANGELO È RIMASTO A LAVORARE PER QUATTRO ANNI, SENZA PERMETTERE A NESSUNO DI ENTRARE, NEANCHE AL PAPA.

DEVI SAPERE CHE IL PAPA ERA COSÌ INSISTENTE E CURIOSO DI VEDERE I LAVORI CHE UN GIORNO, POICHÉ MICHELANGELO AVEVA DETTO CHE ANDAVA A FIRENZE, È ENTRATO DI NASCOSTO. E MICHELANGELO, CHE NON ERA PARTITO, MA AVEVA SOLO FINTO PER CONTROLLARE SE IL PAPA RISPETTAVA IL DIVIETO, QUANDO LO HA SCOPERTO SI È ARRABBIATO MOLTISSIMO, CON IL PAPA!

QUESTA È LA ZONA PROTETTA, QUI I CARDINALI DORMONO, MANGIANO, SI RIUNISCONO IN PREGHIERA PRIMA DELLE VOTAZIONI. MOLTI SONO GIÀ ARRIVATI. VEDI QUEL GRUPPO LÌ A DESTRA?

QUELLI SONO I CARDINALI SUDAMERICANI, SONO TANTI E MOLTO INFLUENTI, L'ELEZIONE DEL NUOVO PAPA DIPENDERÀ ANCHE DAI LORO VOTI. A SINISTRA CI SONO GLI EUROPEI, POI GLI AFRICANI, GLI ASIATICI E I NORDAMERICANI. INFINE IL GRUPPO PIÙ IMPORTANTE, GLI ITALIANI: TUTTI DICONO CHE QUESTA VOLTA TOCCHERÀ A UNO DI LORO.

Habemus papam

E QUELLO CON IL PIZZETTO CHI È? HA UN VISO CONOSCIUTO...

QUELLO È IL CARDINALE STOPPANI, È IL FAVORITO. SE TUTTO VA BENE, LUI DOVREBBE ESSERE IL NUOVO PAPA. MA NON TUTTI LO AMANO.

È UN UOMO ECCEZIONALE: HA AIUTATO TANTISSIMA GENTE, HA COMBATTUTO PER ANNI CONTRO LA MAFIA NEL SUD ITALIA, NON SI È MAI FERMATO DI FRONTE A NESSUNO, NEANCHE DI FRONTE AGLI UOMINI PIÙ POTENTI. PER QUESTO SI È FATTO MOLTI NEMICI.

ZERO SEMBRAVA ESSERE UN GRANDE ESPERTO, SAPEVA TUTTO DI TUTTI E SI MUOVEVA NEI PALAZZI DEL VATICANO CON GRANDE FAMILIARITÀ. IO ERO SORPRESO: VEDEVO IL MIO VECCHIO AMICO, QUELLO CON CUI GIOCAVO DA RAGAZZO, PARLARE DI CARDINALI, CONCLAVE, PAPI, COME DELLA COSA PIÙ NORMALE DEL MONDO.

IN REALTÀ QUELLO ERA UN MONDO PARTICOLARE, AFFASCINANTE E ANCHE STRANO. E LA COSA PIÙ INCREDIBILE ERA CHE ORA ANCH'IO NE FACEVO PARTE. COSÌ LA SERA, TORNATO A CASA, HO COMINCIATO SUBITO A STUDIARE I DOCUMENTI SUI 102 CARDINALI.

UNA DOPO L'ALTRA, SCORREVANO DAVANTI AI MIEI OCCHI LE VITE DI PERSONE PROVENIENTI DA TUTTI I PAESI DEL MONDO. VITE RICCHE DI EVENTI, NOTIZIE CURIOSE, FATTI ECCEZIONALI. SONO RIMASTO TUTTA LA NOTTE A LEGGERE QUELLE BIOGRAFIE. A UN CERTO PUNTO, LA MIA ATTENZIONE SI È FERMATA SUL NUMERO 92: AL CONTRARIO DEGLI ALTRI, PER LUI C'ERA SOLO UNA FOTO E UN NOME. NIENT'ALTRO. NIENTE SUL SUO PAESE, SULLA SUA VITA, LA SUA STORIA. CHI ERA QUEL CARDINALE MISTERIOSO?

n° 092 Cardinale GOTOR

DOMANI, IN VATICANO, COMINCERÀ IL CONCLAVE PER ELEGGERE IL NUOVO PAPA. PARTECIPERANNO CARDINALI DA TUTTO IL MONDO...

FUMATA NERA. CON QUESTO SEGNALE, DOPO OGNI VOTAZIONE, I CARDINALI CHIUSI NEL CONCLAVE COMUNICANO AL MONDO ESTERNO CHE IL NUOVO PAPA NON È STATO ANCORA ELETTO.

RIUNITE IN PIAZZA SAN PIETRO, LA MAGNIFICA PIAZZA CON LA GRANDE BASILICA PROGETTATA DAL GENIO ARCHITETTONICO DEL BERNINI, MIGLIAIA DI PERSONE ASPETTANO LA NOTIZIA. QUEL GIORNO, IL PRIMO DEL NUOVO CONCLAVE, ANCH'IO ERO LÌ.

NELLA PIAZZA, OLTRE AI FEDELI, C'ERANO GIORNALISTI DA TUTTO IL MONDO. MA NON POTEVO IMMAGINARE DI INCONTRARE ANCHE LEI, EFFE, IL MIO AMORE DI UN TEMPO. ORA LAVORAVA PER LA TELEVISIONE. ANCHE LEI ERA GIORNALISTA.

EFFE ERA SEMPRE BELLISSIMA. IN FONDO, MENTRE LA GUARDAVO, MI ACCORGEVO CHE NON L'AVEVO MAI VERAMENTE DIMENTICATA. ERO NERVOSO COSÌ, PER NON PARLARE DI NOI, HO COMINCIATO A PARLARE DI LAVORO.

EFFE, ANCHE TU QUI?

DEVO SCRIVERE LA BIOGRAFIA DEL NUOVO PAPA. PER QUESTO STO STUDIANDO LE VITE DI TUTTI I CARDINALI CHE PARTECIPANO AL CONCLAVE. MA C'È UN CARDINALE SU CUI NON HO NESSUNA INFORMAZIONE. SI CHIAMA GOTOR, LO CONOSCI?

ALEM, QUANTO TEMPO! CI INCONTRIAMO OGNI MORTE DI PAPA!

GOTOR? NO, MAI SENTITO. MA PERDI IL TUO TEMPO. TUTTI SANNO CHI SARÀ IL NUOVO PAPA: È IL CARDINALE STOPPANI. COMUNQUE, SE VUOI POSSIAMO ANDARE A BERE QUALCOSA COSÌ PARLIAMO UN PO' DEI VECCHI TEMPI, TI VA?

ADESSO? VERAMENTE, ADESSO AVREI UN APPUNTAMENTO IMPORTANTE. È PER IL LAVORO DI CUI TI PARLAVO.

BEH, È DAVVERO UN PECCATO CHE TU ABBIA SEMPRE QUALCOSA DI PIÙ IMPORTANTE DI ME. NON IMPORTA... SARÀ PER LA PROSSIMA VOLTA, MAGARI TRA ALTRI DIECI ANNI! CIAO ALEM E IN BOCCA AL LUPO PER IL TUO APPUNTAMENTO!

ANCORA UNA VOLTA, COME UN FILM GIÀ VISTO, LE NOSTRE STRADE ERANO DESTINATE A NON INCONTRARSI.

MA PERCHÉ SONO COSÌ STUPIDO? – PENSAVO – È POSSIBILE CHE CON EFFE FINISCA SEMPRE COSÌ? IN OGNI CASO, IL MIO APPUNTAMENTO ERA DAVVERO IMPORTANTE. ZERO MI AVEVA INVITATO A PRANZO PER PARLARMI. FORSE AVEVA NOTIZIE FRESCHE DAL CONCLAVE...

NESSUN CARDINALE HA OTTENUTO LA MAGGIORANZA, MA È SOLO LA PRIMA VOTAZIONE. DI SOLITO CE NE VOGLIONO ALMENO 4. PENSA CHE PER ELEGGERE GREGORIO X NEL *1200* CI SONO VOLUTI QUASI TRE ANNI! PER FORTUNA QUESTA VOLTA NON SARÀ NECESSARIO TUTTO QUESTO TEMPO.

IL CARDINALE STOPPANI DOVREBBE AVERE PRESTO IL CONSENSO DI TUTTI. ORA MANGIAMO. ASSAGGIA QUESTI SPAGHETTI AL NERO DI SEPPIA... IL NUOVO CUOCO DEL VATICANO È UN VERO ARTISTA!

ZERO AVEVA RAGIONE. QUEGLI SPAGHETTI ERANO ECCEZIONALI. IL NUOVO CUOCO SI CHIAMAVA ALFONSO ED ERA UN NAPOLETANO SIMPATICO E CHIACCHIERONE.

SONO CONTENTO CHE VI PIACCIANO. LI HO CHIAMATI "SPAGHETTI ALLA BORGIA", PERCHÉ NELLA FAMIGLIA BORGIA CI SONO STATI PAPI FAMOSI E POI PERCHÉ LA SALSA DI SEPPIA È SCURA COME IL VELENO CHE USAVA LUCREZIA BORGIA.

15

l'italiano con i fumetti

MA IL NOSTRO ALFONSO FORSE È ANCORA PIÙ BRAVO.

GRAZIE DOTTOR ZERO, TROPPO GENTILE.

SÌ, QUEL PRANZO ERA BUONISSIMO. IO PERÒ NON ERO LÌ SOLO PER MANGIARE. AVEVO INFATTI MOLTE DOMANDE DA FARE A ZERO. LA PRIMA RIGUARDAVA GOTOR, IL MISTERIOSO CARDINALE SU CUI NON AVEVO TROVATO NOTIZIE.

IL CARDINALE GOTOR, SÌ... NON SO MOLTO DI LUI, MA PERCHÉ TI INTERESSA? NON SARÀ CERTO LUI IL NUOVO PAPA. E ORA ASSAGGIA QUESTO VINO, LO PRODUCIAMO QUI IN VATICANO, LO ABBIAMO CHIAMATO "GIUDIZIO UNIVERSALE", PERCHÉ QUANDO LO BEVI È LA FINE DEL MONDO...

ABBIAMO CONTINUATO A MANGIARE E A PARLARE ANCORA FINO A TARDI. MA OGNI VOLTA CHE CERCAVO DI CHIEDERGLI DI GOTOR, ZERO SEMBRAVA SFUGGIRE ALLA DOMANDA. QUEL SUO COMPORTAMENTO NON MI CONVINCEVA.

LA SERA, TORNATO A CASA, HO RICEVUTO UNO STRANO MESSAGGIO.

CIAO ALEM, SONO EFFE. HO BISOGNO DI PARLARTI CON URGENZA. VIENI QUESTA SERA ALLE 11 SUL PONTE DI CASTEL SANT'ANGELO. TI ASPETTO LÌ.

l'italiano con i fumetti

episodio 4

CASTEL SANT'ANGELO DI NOTTE È UNO DEI POSTI DI ROMA CHE PREFERISCO. IL CASTELLO, CHE È STATO PER TANTI SECOLI LA FORTEZZA DEI PAPI E ANCHE UNA PRIGIONE, HA UN'ARIA UN PO' MISTERIOSA. FORSE È PER QUESTO CHE, MENTRE ANDAVO ALL'APPUNTAMENTO CON EFFE, HO COMINCIATO A PENSARE A TUTTE LE STORIE TERRIBILI CHE AVEVO LETTO SU QUEL LUOGO COSÌ PARTICOLARE. PER ESEMPIO, MI SONO RICORDATO DELLA STORIA DEL CARDINALE ORSINI, IMPRIGIONATO NEL CASTELLO DA PAPA ALESSANDRO VI NELL'ANNO 1503.

SECONDO LA LEGGENDA, DOPO AVER SAPUTO LA NOTIZIA, LA MADRE DEL CARDINALE È ANDATA DAL PAPA E GLI HA OFFERTO UNA PERLA PREZIOSISSIMA IN CAMBIO DELLA LIBERAZIONE DEL FIGLIO. IL PAPA, CHE APPARTENEVA ALLA POTENTISSIMA E RICCHISSIMA FAMIGLIA BORGIA (ERA IL PADRE DELLA FAMOSA LUCREZIA), HA ACCETTATO LA PROPOSTA. COSÌ HA PRESO LA PERLA E, FEDELE ALLA SUA PROMESSA, HA RESTITUITO IL CARDINALE ORSINI ALLA MADRE... MORTO!

EFFE MI ASPETTAVA SUL PONTE. ERA AGITATA PER QUALCOSA CHE AVEVA SCOPERTO.

HO AVUTO UNA NOTIZIA RISERVATA. SEMBRA CHE DURANTE IL CONCLAVE SUCCEDERÀ QUALCOSA DI GRAVE, QUALCOSA DI MOLTO BRUTTO... NON TUTTI VOGLIONO CHE IL CARDINALE STOPPANI DIVENTI PAPA.

Habemus papam

QUELLO CHE È SUCCESSO DOPO È INCREDIBILE...

MA QUELLO È IL CARDINALE GOTOR! A QUEST'ORA DOVREBBE ESSERE CHIUSO NEL CONCLAVE, NESSUNO DEI CARDINALI PUÒ USCIRE!

GOTOR ERA SCESO DA UNA MACCHINA NERA, MOLTO SIMILE A QUELLA DEL MIO SOGNO, DENTRO C'ERANO DUE UOMINI, ANCHE LORO LI AVEVO TGIÀ VISTI NEL SOGNO. I QUATTRO HANNO PARLATO UN PO'!

POI IL CARDINALE E ZERO HANNO SALUTATO I DUE UOMINI E SONO ANDATI VIA INSIEME.

STANNO ENTRANDO IN UN PASSAGGIO SEGRETO, ANDIAMO ANCHE NOI.

ABBIAMO APERTO LA PORTA NASCOSTA NEL MURO E CI SIAMO TROVATI IN UNA GALLERIA BUIA. ERAVAMO SOTTO IL FAMOSO PASSO DEL BORGHETTO, LA VIA CHE I PAPI AVEVANO UTILIZZATO PER SECOLI PER ANDARE IN SEGRETO DA SAN PIETRO A CASTEL SANT'ANGELO QUANDO ROMA ERA IN PERICOLO.

EFFE, ASPETTA... PUÒ ESSERE PERICOLOSO!

DAI ALEM, MUOVITI! NON DOBBIAMO PERDERLI!

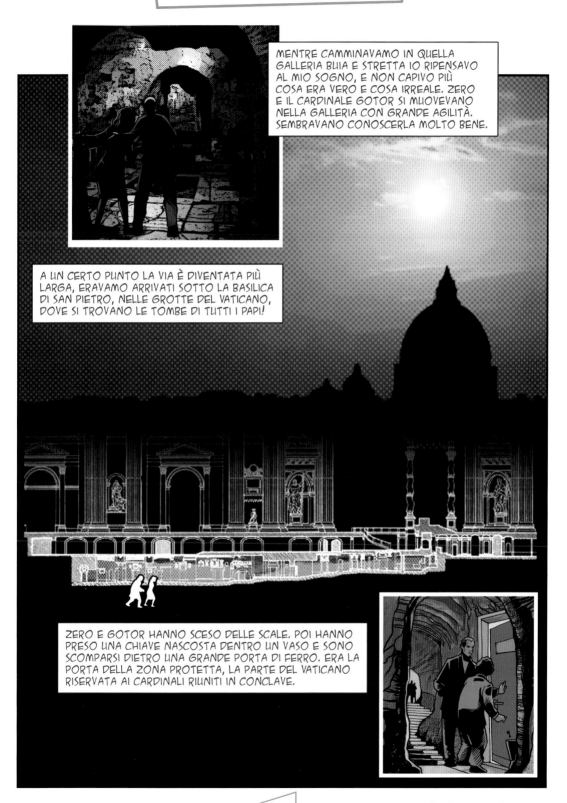

MENTRE CAMMINAVAMO IN QUELLA GALLERIA BUIA E STRETTA IO RIPENSAVO AL MIO SOGNO, E NON CAPIVO PIÙ COSA ERA VERO E COSA IRREALE. ZERO E IL CARDINALE GOTOR SI MUOVEVANO NELLA GALLERIA CON GRANDE AGILITÀ. SEMBRAVANO CONOSCERLA MOLTO BENE.

A UN CERTO PUNTO LA VIA È DIVENTATA PIÙ LARGA, ERAVAMO ARRIVATI SOTTO LA BASILICA DI SAN PIETRO, NELLE GROTTE DEL VATICANO, DOVE SI TROVANO LE TOMBE DI TUTTI I PAPI!

ZERO E GOTOR HANNO SCESO DELLE SCALE. POI HANNO PRESO UNA CHIAVE NASCOSTA DENTRO UN VASO E SONO SCOMPARSI DIETRO UNA GRANDE PORTA DI FERRO. ERA LA PORTA DELLA ZONA PROTETTA, LA PARTE DEL VATICANO RISERVATA AI CARDINALI RIUNITI IN CONCLAVE.

l'italiano con i fumetti

QUELLA NOTTE, I CARDINALI SI ERANO RIUNITI IN PREGHIERA PER CERCARE L'ISPIRAZIONE DIVINA. POCO PRIMA, INFATTI, C'ERA STATA UN'ALTRA FUMATA NERA. ERA LA TERZA DI QUELLA LUNGA GIORNATA.

ANCHE QUESTA VOLTA IL CARDINALE STOPPANI ERA STATO IL PIÙ VOTATO. TUTTAVIA, IL SUO NOME SEMBRAVA NON RIUSCIRE A CONVINCERE TUTTI. E ZERO, CHE ERA APPENA RIENTRATO DOPO L'USCITA NOTTURNA CON IL CARDINALE GOTOR, AVEVA CHIESTO DI PARLARGLI.

EMINENZA, SIAMO MOLTO VICINI ALLA SUA ELEZIONE. PERÒ, MANCA ANCORA QUALCOSA... FORSE, SE MI POSSO PERMETTERE, SERVIREBBE UN PO' PIÙ DI MODERAZIONE. DOVREBBE PARLARE AGLI ALTRI CARDINALI E DIRE CHE QUELLO CHE SI DICE SU DI LEI NON È VERO. IL NUOVO PAPA DOVRÀ ESSERE UNA PERSONA CHE PORTA PACE, NON GUERRA...

COSA VUOLE DIRE DOTTOR ZERO? NON CAPISCO. NELLA MIA VITA IO HO SEMPRE COMBATTUTO LE INGIUSTIZIE, E CONTINUERÒ A FARLO ANCHE SE SARÒ PAPA. QUESTO PER LEI SIGNIFICA PORTARE LA GUERRA? FORSE LEI NON SA CHE LA MAFIA HA PROVATO AD UCCIDERMI PIÙ DI UNA VOLTA, MA IO NON MI SONO MAI FERMATO DI FRONTE A NIENTE.

SCUSA EFFE, VOGLIO DIRTI CHE IO NON SONO ASSOLUTAMENTE D'ACCORDO SU QUELLO CHE STIAMO FACENDO...

INTANTO, IO E EFFE ERAVAMO RIUSCITI A ENTRARE CON LA CHIAVE DEL VASO. O MEGLIO, EFFE ERA ENTRATA, ED IO L'AVEVO SEGUITA.

RILASSATI ALEM. SENTI CHE BELLA QUESTA MUSICA. È UN CANTO GREGORIANO. LO SAI CHE NEL CANTO GREGORIANO NON CI SONO GLI STRUMENTI? È COSÌ BELLO CHE NON SERVONO. VIENI, ENTRIAMO QUI DENTRO.

23

SIAMO ARRIVATI IN UNA SALA PIENA DI LIBRI. UNA PARTE ERA DEDICATA AL CONCLAVE. C'ERANO DOCUMENTI ANTICHI ED ALTRI PIÙ MODERNI. UN PICCOLO DOSSIER RIGUARDAVA PROPRIO L'ULTIMO CONCLAVE.

COSA HAI TROVATO?

È LA LISTA DI TUTTI I CARDINALI PARTECIPANTI. QUI C'È SCRITTO CHE SONO 101, NON 102!

HO CONTROLLATO TUTTI I NOMI. COME IMMAGINAVO, QUELLO DI GOTOR NON C'ERA. POI EFFE HA VISTO QUALCOSA...

GUARDA QUESTA FOTO: TI RICORDA QUALCUNO?

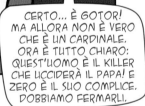

ALFA 331

CERTO... È GOTOR! MA ALLORA NON È VERO CHE È UN CARDINALE. ORA È TUTTO CHIARO; QUEST'UOMO È IL KILLER CHE UCCIDERÀ IL PAPA! E ZERO È IL SUO COMPLICE. DOBBIAMO FERMARLI.

ALL'IMPROVVISO, ABBIAMO SENTITO DEI PASSI. STAVA ARRIVANDO QUALCUNO. ERANO LE GUARDIE SVIZZERE, LA POLIZIA DEL VATICANO.

CUCINA

VIENI, NASCONDIAMOCI QUI.

25

ORMAI ERA MATTINA. IO E EFFE, NASCOSTI IN CUCINA, ABBIAMO SENTITO DELLE GRIDA DALLA PIAZZA.

Evviva! Alleluia! CLAP CLAP

COSA? SENTI CHE BUONI QUESTI CORNETTI...

ALEM, GUARDA! C'È LA FUMATA BIANCA, È STATO ELETTO IL PAPA!

MA LASCIA STARE LA COLAZIONE, NON È IL MOMENTO... SE IL NUOVO PAPA FOSSE STOPPANI, SAREBBE IN PERICOLO. GOTOR E ZERO VOGLIONO UCCIDERLO. DOBBIAMO FARE QUALCOSA.

ABBIAMO ATTRAVERSATO UN CORRIDOIO E SIAMO ENTRATI IN UN'ALTRA PARTE DELLA CUCINA. QUI IL CUOCO ALFONSO STAVA PREPARANDO LE COLAZIONI PER I CARDINALI.

QUESTA È PER IL CARDINALE STOPPANI, È LUI IL NUOVO PAPA. GLIELA PORTO IO.

ALFONSO È USCITO CON LA COLAZIONE PER IL PAPA. PROPRIO IN QUEL MOMENTO È ARRIVATO ZERO.

E VOI COSA FATE QUI? GUARDIE ARRESTATELI!

Habemus papam

l'italiano con i fumetti

FINALMENTE ERA TUTTO CHIARO: IL KILLER ERA ALFONSO, NON GOTOR. COME UN MODERNO BORGIA, FORSE ISPIRATO DALLE TERRIBILI E AFFASCINANTI STORIE DI QUEI LUOGHI, IL CUOCO AVEVA MESSO UN VELENO NEL CAFFÈ DEL PAPA PER UCCIDERLO. ZERO CI HA SPIEGATO TUTTO:

QUANDO IN VATICANO ABBIAMO SAPUTO CHE ALCUNE ORGANIZZAZIONI CRIMINALI VOLEVANO UCCIDERE IL FAVORITO DEL CONCLAVE, IL CARDINALE STOPPANI, ABBIAMO PENSATO A UN PIANO DI PROTEZIONE. COSÌ ABBIAMO DECISO DI METTERE VICINO AL FUTURO PAPA UN "ANGELO CUSTODE", IL CARDINALE GOTOR.

PER QUESTO SU DI LUI NON HAI TROVATO NOTIZIE, IL CARDINALE GOTOR IN REALTÀ È L'AGENTE RENZI, CHE LAVORA PER I SERVIZI DI SICUREZZA VATICANI. QUESTA MATTINA, DOPO CHE I CARDINALI HANNO ELETTO IL CARDINALE STOPPANI, ALFONSO HA DECISO DI ENTRARE IN AZIONE, METTENDO IL VELENO NEL CAFFÈ.

MA IO, PARLANDO CON VOI, HO CAPITO TUTTO E SONO CORSO AD AVVERTIRE RENZI, CHE È RIUSCITO A FERMARLO APPENA IN TEMPO. GRAZIE A DIO, IL PAPA È SALVO. E ORA POSSIAMO FINALMENTE ANNUNCIARE AL MONDO LA BUONA NOTIZIA.

PIAZZA SAN PIETRO, UN'ORA DOPO. MIGLIAIA DI PERSONE ASCOLTANO LA BUONA NOTIZIA: IL MONDO HA UN NUOVO PAPA.

NUNTIO VOBIS GAUDIUM MAGNUM: HABEMUS PAPAM!*

CHE FAI STASERA?

HO PRESO LA MANO DI EFFE E L'HO STRETTA FORTE. QUALCOSA DI NUOVO E DI BELLO STAVA INIZIANDO ANCHE PER NOI. MA QUESTA È UN'ALTRA STORIA...

FINE

*TRADUZIONE: VI ANNUNCIO UNA GRANDE E BELLA NOTIZIA: ABBIAMO UN (NUOVO) PAPA.

l'italiano con i fumetti

uno

Leggi il primo episodio e rispondi alle domande.

1. Come si chiama l'amico di Alem?
- ☐ a. Zero.
- ☐ b. Paolo.
- ☐ c. Effe.

2. Perché Alem vuole andare alla stazione di polizia?
- ☐ a. Perché ha perso il passaporto.
- ☐ b. Per consegnare i documenti che gli ha dato Zero.
- ☐ c. Per denunciare una macchina nera.

3. Chi ha lasciato un messaggio sulla segreteria telefonica di Alem?
- ☐ a. Zero.
- ☐ b. La polizia.
- ☐ c. Effe.

4. Chi aspetta Alem in piazza San Pietro?
- ☐ a. Zero.
- ☐ b. La polizia.
- ☐ c. Effe.

due

Leggi ancora il primo episodio, poi riscrivi le frasi usando i pronomi, come nell'esempio.

1. Effe aspetta Alem in piazza San Pietro.
   Effe lo aspetta.

2. Due uomini nella macchina nera seguono Alem.
   Due uomini _____

3. Zero non saluta Alem.
   Zero _____

4. Zero consegna una busta a Alem.
   Zero _____

5. Due uomini nella macchina nera sparano a Effe.
   Due uomini _____

6. Alem vuole andare dalla polizia.
   _____ andare.

Piazza San Pietro

Piazza San Pietro non si trova in Italia: per la precisione, infatti, la piazza fa parte di Città del Vaticano, il più piccolo Stato indipendente del mondo.

Piazza San Pietro è un notevole esempio di architettura barocca: con la sua forma ovale e il famoso colonnato di Gian Lorenzo Bernini che la circonda, è il cuore del cattolicesimo e accoglie ogni anno milioni di visitatori, turisti e pellegrini (cioè viaggiatori per ragioni religiose), che visitano il Vaticano per vedere il Papa o semplicemente per entrare nella basilica, o fanno pazientemente la fila per ammirare i capolavori dei Musei Vaticani.

tre — *Completa il testo con i pronomi della lista.*

| io | lei | lo | me | mi | mi | mi | si | ti | ti | tu |

_____ chiamo Alem. Strano nome, _____ so... Ho sempre avuto problemi per questo. _____ ricordo quando avevo 6 anni, il mio primo giorno di scuola.

Maestra: No caro, il tuo nome non _____ scrive così... _____ _____ chiami Alem, non Mela!

E questo sono _____ a vent'anni. La ragazza è Effe, il mio grande amore. Con _____ non sono mai riuscito a cogliere l'occasione giusta.

Effe: Ciao Alem, come stai? _____ va di uscire con _____ stasera?

Alem: Stasera? _____ dispiace non posso. Devo studiare, domani ho un esame importante. Facciamo domani sera?

Effe: No, domani esco con Paolo!

quattro

Completa il testo coniugando i verbi tra parentesi al passato prossimo, all'imperfetto o al trapassato prossimo.

Una sera, mentre (*uscire*) _____ dal giornale, (*incontrare*)
_____ Zero, il mio vecchio amico. Non lo (*vedere*) _____
da un sacco di tempo, ma lui non mi (*salutare*) _____ neanche, mi (*dare*)
_____ una strana busta e (*andarsene*) _____.
Ed è così che (*iniziare*) _____ questa assurda storia. La busta (*contenere*)
_____ dei documenti scritti in una lingua che non (*conoscere*)
_____. Poi (*esserci*) _____ una lunga lista di nomi
sconosciuti, ma la cosa più strana (*essere*) _____ che ogni pagina (*essere*)
_____ piena di scritte e timbri che (*dire*) _____ TOP SECRET,
SERVIZI SEGRETI, INTELLIGENCE, ecc.
Non (*sapere*) _____ cosa fare, mi (*fare*) _____ mille
domande. Perché Zero mi (*dare*) _____ quei documenti? Perché (*scappare*)
_____? Alla fine (*uscire*) _____ dall'ufficio per portare tutto alla
polizia, ma (*accorgersi*) _____ che qualcuno mi (*stare*) _____
seguendo, (*essere*) _____ una macchina nera, dietro di me.

Riassunto episodio 2

Alem è un giornalista che una sera incontra per caso un vecchio amico, Zero. Senza neanche salutarlo, Zero gli dà una strana busta e gli dice di andare a mezzanotte in piazza San Pietro.
Alem apre la busta e capisce che si tratta di documenti segreti e decide di portare tutto alla polizia. Ma per strada una macchina nera lo segue: riesce però a scappare e ritorna a casa. Lì trova un messaggio telefonico di Effe, il suo grande amore di gioventù. Effe ha bisogno di vederlo urgentemente.
A mezzanotte Alem trova in piazza San Pietro proprio Effe, che gli chiede i documenti segreti. In quel momento però arriva di nuovo la macchina nera con due uomini dentro. I due sparano e feriscono Effe. Ricomincia l'inseguimento, i due uomini armati fermano Alem e gli chiedono violentemente i documenti. Alem si sveglia terrorizzato: era tutto un sogno!
Ma mentre si fa la barba, il telefono squilla: è Zero, il vecchio amico che Alem ha sognato quella stessa notte.

uno

Leggi il secondo episodio e rispondi alle domande.

1. Che lavoro fa Zero?
- ☐ a. È un poliziotto.
- ☐ b. È diventato prete.
- ☐ c. Lavora in Vaticano.

2. Quale lavoro propone Zero a Alem?
- ☐ a. Scrivere la biografia del nuovo Papa.
- ☐ b. Fare indagini sul nuovo Papa.
- ☐ c. Cercare Effe.

3. Dove si svolgeranno le votazioni per l'elezione del nuovo Papa?
- ☐ a. Nelle stanze di Raffaello.
- ☐ b. Nella Cappella Sistina.
- ☐ c. Dentro Castel Sant'Angelo.

4. Chi è il cardinale Stoppani?
- ☐ a. Il segretario particolare del precedente Papa.
- ☐ b. Il favorito a diventare il nuovo Papa.
- ☐ c. Un uomo sospettato di avere contatti con la mafia.

due

Leggi ancora il secondo episodio, poi ricostruisci le frasi.

Il cardinale Gotor	ha ricevuto una proposta di lavoro non rifiutabile.
Il cardinale Stoppani	non vede Alem da molto tempo.
Zero	per quattro anni non ha permesso a nessuno di entrare nella Cappella Sistina.
Alem	ha combattuto per anni contro la mafia.
Michelangelo	è una figura misteriosa.

tre

Completa il testo con le preposizioni.

La più famosa cappella ___ mondo deve il suo nome a papa Sisto IV, che ___ 1473 fa iniziare i lavori ___ la ricostruzione e la decorazione ___ sala dove si dovevano svolgere le cerimonie più importanti ___ corte papale. Lavorano agli affreschi importanti artisti ___ epoca come il Perugino, Botticelli e il Ghirlandaio.

Nel 1508 papa Giulio II chiama il grande artista Michelangelo ___ decorare il soffitto (la volta) ___ cappella. Michelangelo finisce la sua opera ___ 1512, lavorando ___ condizioni molto difficili, per la posizione scomoda e per non pochi problemi tecnici.

Poco più ___ vent'anni dopo, papa Clemente VII vuole di nuovo Michelangelo ___ affrescare la parete di fondo ___ il Giudizio Universale, che Michelangelo termina sotto il successore di Clemente, il papa Paolo III.

quattro

Guarda la fotografia e scrivi le parole della lista al posto giusto.

cupola   colonnato   obelisco   piazza   scalinata   statua

a. _____   b. _____   c. _____

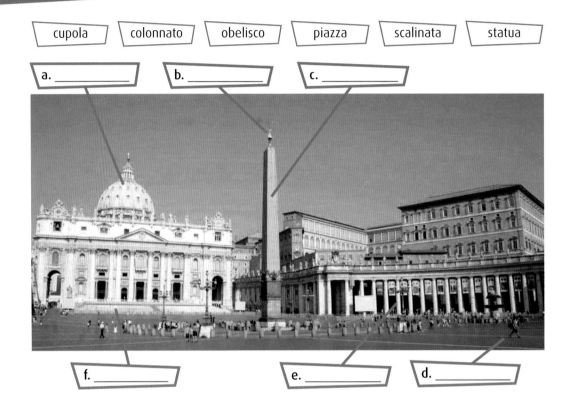

f. _____   e. _____   d. _____

Riassunto episodio 3

Zero, diventato un importante funzionario del Vaticano, ha chiamato Alem per fargli una proposta di lavoro: dopo la fine del conclave servirà una biografia del nuovo Papa e Alem sembra la persona più adatta a scriverla. In una busta Alem trova il contratto e i documenti con le informazioni su tutti i cardinali partecipanti.
Poi Zero mostra ad Alem alcuni cardinali e parla del favorito, il cardinale Stoppani, un uomo coraggioso che non tutti però amano.
Alem inizia così a lavorare sulle biografie dei cardinali, tutte molto dettagliate tranne una, quella del cardinale Gotor: per lui, solo una foto e il nome. Perché tanto mistero?

uno | *Leggi il terzo episodio e rispondi alle domande.*

1. Che significato ha la fumata nera durante il conclave?
- ☐ **a.** Il nuovo Papa è stato eletto.
- ☐ **b.** Il nuovo Papa non è stato eletto.
- ☐ **c.** Il conclave è finito.

2. Con chi ha appuntamento Alem a pranzo?
- ☐ **a.** Con Zero.
- ☐ **b.** Con Effe.
- ☐ **c.** Con il cardinale Stoppani.

3. Il cuoco ha scelto il nome "spaghetti alla Borgia" per la pasta al nero di seppia perché:
- ☐ **a.** Borgia era il nome di una famiglia di pescatori.
- ☐ **b.** Nella famiglia Borgia ci sono stati cuochi famosi.
- ☐ **c.** Il colore della salsa di seppia è scura come il veleno che usava Lucrezia Borgia.

4. Cosa risponde Zero alle domande di Alem riguardo al cardinale Gotor?
- ☐ **a.** Non risponde.
- ☐ **b.** Consegna a Alem alcuni documenti sul cardinale.
- ☐ **c.** Dice che Gotor è un appassionato di vino.

due | *Leggi ancora il terzo episodio, poi ricostruisci le frasi.*

Alem	fa la giornalista.
Alem	deve andare a pranzo con Zero.
Alfonso	è convinto che il nuovo Papa sarà il cardinale Stoppani.
Effe	viene da Napoli.
Zero	sfugge alle domande di Alem.
Zero	ha dei dubbi sul comportamento di Zero.

La famiglia Borgia

Di origini spagnole, la famiglia Borgia è stata una delle più potenti e importanti in Italia tra il XV e il XVI secolo. L'occasione per trasferirsi da Valencia a Roma è l'elezione a papa del cardinale Alonso Borgia nel 1455 (papa Callisto III). Anche uno dei suoi nipoti, Rodrigo, viene eletto papa nel 1492 con il nome di Alessandro VI, diventando uno dei papi simbolo della corruzione e del cosiddetto "nepotismo", cioè il favorire i parenti e dare loro importanti ruoli politici e sociali: non solo nipoti, ma anche figli, dato che Rodrigo, sebbene cardinale e poi papa, aveva sei figli avuti da tre donne diverse.
Tra i suoi figli si ricordano soprattutto il crudele Cesare Borgia, detto il "Valentino" - citato anche da Machiavelli come esempio di spietatezza – e Lucrezia Borgia, passata alla storia (ma soprattutto nella leggenda) come amante dello stesso papa e abile nell'usare il veleno per eliminare i suoi nemici.

tre

Leggi i testi e fai attenzione alle espressioni evidenziate in blu. Poi abbina i fumetti alle espressioni corrispondenti.

a. Buona fortuna!   **b.** È ottimo!   **c.** Molto raramente.

1. EFFE, ANCHE TU QUI?

ALEM, QUANTO TEMPO! CI INCONTRIAMO OGNI MORTE DI PAPA!

2. ADESSO? VERAMENTE, ADESSO AVREI UN APPUNTAMENTO IMPORTANTE. È PER IL LAVORO DI CUI TI PARLAVO.

BEH, È DAVVERO UN PECCATO CHE TU ABBIA SEMPRE QUALCOSA DI PIÙ IMPORTANTE DI ME. NON IMPORTA... SARÀ PER LA PROSSIMA VOLTA, MAGARI TRA ALTRI DIECI ANNI! CIAO ALEM E IN BOCCA AL LUPO PER IL TUO APPUNTAMENTO!

3. IL CARDINALE GOTOR, SÌ... NON SO MOLTO DI LUI, MA PERCHÉ TI INTERESSA? NON SARÀ CERTO LUI IL NUOVO PAPA. E ORA ASSAGGIA QUESTO VINO, LO PRODUCIAMO QUI IN VATICANO, LO ABBIAMO CHIAMATO "GIUDIZIO UNIVERSALE", PERCHÉ QUANDO LO BEVI È LA FINE DEL MONDO...

quattro

Completa le battute con i verbi della lista.

abbia	ci sono stati	è	importa	piacciano
potrebbe	sarà	sia	sono	sono

Beh, _____ davvero un peccato che tu _____ sempre qualcosa di più importante di me. Non _____ ... _____ per la prossima volta, magari tra altri dieci anni.

Li ho chiamati "spaghetti alla Borgia" perché nella famiglia Borgia _____ papi famosi. _____ contento che vi _____.

Qualcuno _____ pensare che in un'occasione così importante come il conclave il cibo _____ l'ultimo dei pensieri dei cardinali. Invece anche loro _____ uomini come noi.

Riassunto episodio 3

In piazza San Pietro Alem incontra Effe, una ragazza di cui era innamorato da giovane: anche lei è giornalista ed è lì per lavoro. Effe lo invita a bere qualcosa, ma lui rifiuta perché deve pranzare con Zero in Vaticano. Mentre mangiano, Zero racconta ad Alem curiosità e notizie storiche sui papi del passato e gli presenta il nuovo cuoco del Vaticano, Alfonso, un artista della cucina. Alem cerca di sapere qualcosa di più su Gotor, ma Zero evita sempre l'argomento e Alem sospetta qualcosa.
Tornato a casa, trova un messaggio di Effe che chiede di vederlo con urgenza sul ponte di Castel Sant'Angelo.

uno — *Leggi il quarto episodio e rispondi alle domande.*

1. Dove hanno appuntamento Alem e Effe?
- ☐ a. Davanti alla Basilica di San Pietro.
- ☐ b. Davanti a Castel Sant'Angelo.
- ☐ c. Nei sotterranei del Vaticano.

2. Perché Effe vuole parlare con Alem?
- ☐ a. Perché vuole invitarlo a cena fuori.
- ☐ b. Perché ha bisogno del suo aiuto.
- ☐ c. Perché vuole parlare con Gotor.

3. Chi incontra Gotor davanti a Castel Sant'Angelo?
- ☐ a. Il cardinale Stoppani.
- ☐ b. Il cardinale Orsini.
- ☐ c. Zero.

4. Perché Alem e Effe entrano nel passaggio segreto?
- ☐ a. Perché vogliono visitare le tombe dei papi.
- ☐ b. Perché stanno seguendo il cardinale Gotor e Zero.
- ☐ c. Perché stanno scappando dai due uomini nella macchina nera.

due — *Leggi ancora il quarto episodio, poi ricostruisci le frasi.*

Effe	ha appuntamento con Zero.
Alem	entra in un passaggio segreto con il cardinale Gotor.
Il cardinale Gotor	non si fida di Zero.
Zero	ha ricevuto una notizia riservata riguardo al conclave.

Castel Sant'Angelo e il passo del Borghetto

Molto più del Colosseo e di altri monumenti più famosi, Castel Sant'Angelo rappresenta la città di Roma e l'ha seguita nei tanti cambiamenti dall'antichità a oggi.

Nasce come sepolcro dell'imperatore Adriano, ma dal 403 d.C. inizia una "seconda vita" come fortificazione per proteggere Roma dai barbari. Nel medioevo avere il controllo sul castello significava controllare la città e Castel Sant'Angelo diventa il centro delle rivalità tra le più potenti famiglie di Roma, tra cui gli Orsini.

È proprio un papa Orsini - Niccolò III - a far realizzare il Passo del Borghetto (detto anche il Corridore), che collega il Vaticano al Castello: si tratta di 800 metri sotto terra che i pontefici usavano in caso di pericolo. Per questo motivo Castel Sant'Angelo è legato da secoli alle vicende del Vaticano e dei papi.

(adattato da www.castelsantangelo.com)

tre

Completa il testo con le parole della lista.

famosa	fedele	imprigionato	misteriosa	morto	particolare

potentissima	preziosissima	ricchissima	tanti	terribili

Castel Sant'Angelo di notte è uno dei posti di Roma che preferisco. Il castello, che è stato
per _____ secoli la fortezza dei Papi e anche una prigione, ha un'aria un po'
_____ . Forse è per questo che mentre andavo all'appuntamento con Effe ho
cominciato a pensare a tutte le storie _____ che avevo letto su quel luogo
così _____. Per esempio, mi sono ricordato della storia del cardinale Orsini,
_____ nel castello da papa Alessandro VI nell'anno 1503.
Secondo la leggenda, dopo aver saputo la notizia, la madre del cardinale è andata dal Papa
e gli ha offerto una perla _____ in cambio della liberazione del figlio. Il Papa
che apparteneva alla _____ e _____ famiglia Borgia (era il
padre della _____ Lucrezia), ha accettato la proposta, così ha preso la perla
e, _____ alla sua promessa, ha restituito il cardinale Orsini alla madre...
_____ !

quattro

*Durante l'episodio 4, Effe dice: "Parli del diavolo e spuntano le corna". Cosa
significa? In italiano ci sono altri modi di dire dove compare il diavolo.
Abbina le espressioni idiomatiche al loro significato.*

1. Parli del diavolo e spuntano le corna.
2. Fare l'avvocato del diavolo.
3. Fare il diavolo a quattro.
4. Avere un diavolo per capello.
5. Essere come il diavolo e l'acqua santa.
6. ... Se il diavolo non ci mette la coda!

a. Fare di tutto per ottenere qualcosa.
b. ... Se non capitano imprevisti!
c. Arriva in quel momento la persona di cui si parla.
d. Due persone con caratteri completamente diversi.
e. Cercare i possibili punti deboli di un ragionamento.
f. Essere molto arrabbiato.

Cinque *Completa le battute del dialogo mettendo in ordine le parole in ogni frase mancante e coniugando i verbi sottolineati al modo e tempo opportuni.*

| cardinale | che | diventare | il | Papa | Stoppani | tutti | volere |

Effe: Ho avuto una notizia riservata. Sembra che durante il conclave succederà qualcosa di grave, qualcosa di molto brutto... non _____ _____

_____ _____ _____ _____

_____ _____ .

| a | aiutarmi | capire | che | meglio | pensare | potere |

Il suo programma va contro gli interessi di qualche potente organizzazione. Tu ora lavori per il Vaticano. _____ _____ _____

_____ _____ _____ _____ .

| a | continuare | non | rispondermi |

Alem: Io in Vaticano conosco solo Zero, il mio vecchio amico. Lui ora lavora là, è una persona importante. Potrei chiedergli se sa qualcosa di questa storia, ma forse è meglio di no. Non mi fido molto di lui.

Gli ho chiesto informazioni sul cardinale Gotor, ma _____ _____

_____ _____ . C'è qualcosa di strano nel suo comportamento.

Riassunto episodio 4

Arrivato davanti a Castel Sant'Angelo, Alem trova Effe che gli rivela una notizia riservata, secondo la quale accadrà qualcosa di brutto durante il conclave. Mentre Alem pensa a cosa fare, Effe vede Zero camminare da solo verso Castel Sant'Angelo. Effe e Alem decidono di seguirlo e vedono che si incontra con il cardinale Gotor, uscito da un'auto simile a quella del sogno di Alem.
Zero e Gotor entrano poi in un passaggio segreto, il passo del Borghetto, che collega Castel Sant'Angelo con il Vaticano. Alem e Effe li seguono.

uno   *Leggi il quinto episodio e rispondi alle domande.*

1. Perché Zero parla con il cardinale Stoppani?
- ☐ **a.** Per comunicargli che è stato eletto papa.
- ☐ **b.** Per consigliargli di parlare con gli altri cardinali.
- ☐ **c.** Per chiedergli un consiglio.

2. Quali rapporti ha il cardinale Stoppani con la mafia?
- ☐ **a.** È sospettato di essere un mafioso.
- ☐ **b.** Ha sempre combattuto la mafia.
- ☐ **c.** Ha tentato di uccidere alcuni mafiosi.

3. Come hanno fatto Effe e Alem ad entrare nei sotterranei del Vaticano?
- ☐ **a.** Hanno preso la chiave in un vaso.
- ☐ **b.** Sono stati aiutati da Zero.
- ☐ **c.** Hanno seguito il cardinale Stoppani.

4. Cosa trova Alem alla fine dell'episodio?
- ☐ **a.** Una mappa degli appartamenti del papa.
- ☐ **b.** Un documento sui dipinti di Raffaello.
- ☐ **c.** Un dossier sul conclave.

due   *Leggi ancora il quinto episodio, poi ricostruisci le frasi.*

Effe	è un impostore.
Alem	prende la chiave nel vaso.
Il cardinale Gotor	ha paura di essere scoperto.
Zero	ha subito diversi attentati mafiosi.
Il cardinale Stoppani	dà un consiglio al cardinale Stoppani.

A ogni... dimissione di papa!

Abbiamo visto che l'espressione "a ogni morte di Papa" indica un fatto che avviene molto raramente. Tuttavia ormai potremmo anche dire "a ogni dimissione di Papa": infatti, con le dimissioni di papa Benedetto XVI, che il 28 febbraio 2013 ha deciso di tornare ad essere cardinale Ratzinger, sono storicamente solo sette i papi che hanno rinunciato alla carica pontificia.

Il primo è stato papa Clemente I nel 97 d.C., nel 235 papa Ponziano. Bisogna aspettare il 537 per avere un altro papa dimissionario, papa Silverio, seguito molto dopo da papa Benedetto IX (1045). Del 1294 è il famoso "gran rifiuto" di Celestino V citato anche da Dante nella Commedia, mentre Gregorio XII rinuncia nel 1415.

tre Osserva le opere e abbinale all'autore corrispondente, come nell'esempio.

a. Michelangelo   **b.** Raffaello   **c.** Leonardo

1. Ritratto di dama con liocorno

2. Studio sui gatti (dettaglio)

3. La battaglia di Anghiari

4. La creazione di Adamo

5. Dama con ermellino

6. Il Tondo Doni

1/ _b_ ; 2/___ ; 3/___ ; 4/___ ; 5/___ ; 6/___ .

l'italiano con i fumetti

quattro *Trasforma i testi dal discorso diretto a quello indiretto, come nell'esempio.*

discorso diretto	discorso indiretto
Effe: Cosa hai trovato?	Effe ha chiesto ad Alem _____ _____ _____
Alem: È la lista di tutti i cardinali partecipanti. Qui c'è scritto che sono 101, non 102!	Alem ha detto a Effe che _____ _____ _____

Riassunto episodio 5

Rientrato in Vaticano, Zero consiglia al cardinale Stoppani di essere più moderato, ma il cardinale rifiuta con decisione. Intanto Effe e Alem sono arrivati nelle famose "stanze di Raffaello", decorate con gli affreschi del grande artista. In una sala piena di libri, Alem trova la lista dei cardinali partecipanti al conclave e scopre che il cardinale Gotor è un impostore, probabilmente un killer.
All'arrivo di due guardie svizzere, Effe e Alem si nascondono nelle cucine.

uno   *Leggi il sesto episodio e rispondi alle domande.*

1. Cosa è successo la mattina, mentre Effe e Alem erano in cucina?
- ☐ **a.** È stato eletto il nuovo Papa.
- ☐ **b.** C'è stata una nuova fumata nera.
- ☐ **c.** Effe aveva fame.

2. Cosa vedono Effe e Alem?
- ☐ **a.** I cardinali che fanno colazione.
- ☐ **b.** Alfonso che sta mangiando un cornetto.
- ☐ **c.** Alfonso che mette qualcosa nella colazione di Stoppani.

3. Perché Zero corre via e lascia soli Alem e Effe?
- ☐ **a.** Perché ha capito che il Papa è in pericolo.
- ☐ **b.** Perché vuole arrestare Gotor.
- ☐ **c.** Perché vuole vedere il nuovo Papa.

4. Chi è in realtà Gotor?
- ☐ **a.** Un complice di Alfonso.
- ☐ **b.** Un cardinale esperto nell'uso delle armi.
- ☐ **c.** Un agente di sicurezza.

due   *Leggi ancora il sesto episodio, poi ricostruisci le frasi.*

Alfonso	è salutato dalla folla di San Pietro.
Alem	mette del veleno nel caffè del nuovo Papa.
Zero	fa arrestare Alem e Effe.
Gotor	ferisce Alfonso e lo arresta.
Zero	spiega tutto a Effe e Alem.
Il cardinale Stoppani	crede che l'assassino sia Zero.

Fumata bianca e fumata nera: forse non tutti sanno che...

Sono famose le fumate che si alzano dal caminetto appositamente allestito durante il conclave: ogni due votazioni con esito negativo, infatti, le schede sono bruciate in una stufa appositamente allestita nella Cappella Sistina. Per ottenere il caratteristico fumo nero si bruciano le schede assieme a una sostanza chimica che dà alla fumata il colore scuro. Quando, finalmente, la votazione ha esito positivo, le schede vengono comunque bruciate, ma la sostanza chimica usata questa volta produce la celebre fumata bianca.

tre

Completa il testo con le parole e i verbi mancanti.

Zero racconta come era stata organizzata la protezione del cardinale Stoppani dai servizi di sicurezza.

sicurezza	avvertire	custode	criminali	azione

annunciare	salvo	protezione	agente

"Quando in Vaticano abbiamo saputo che alcune organizzazioni _____ volevano uccidere il favorito del conclave, il cardinale Stoppani, abbiamo pensato a un piano di _____. Così, abbiamo deciso di mettere vicino al futuro Papa un "angelo _____", il cardinale Gotor. Per questo su di lui non hai trovato notizie, il cardinale Gotor in realtà è l'_____ Renzi, che lavora per i servizi di _____ vaticani. Questa mattina, dopo che i cardinali hanno eletto il cardinale Stoppani, Alfonso ha deciso di entrare in _____, mettendo il veleno nel caffè.
Ma io parlando con voi ho capito tutto e sono corso ad _____ Renzi, che è riuscito a fermarlo appena in tempo. Grazie a Dio, il Papa è _____. E ora possiamo finalmente _____ al mondo la buona notizia.

quattro

Completa le frasi e scrivi i verbi con il tempo corretto (attivo e passivo).

1. Dopo aver saputo che Stoppani (*eleggere*) _____ papa,

2. Zero vuole fare arrestare Alem

3. Zero corre ad avvertire Renzi

4. Alem e Effe avevano sempre creduto

a. che Gotor (*essere*) _____ un assassino.

b. perché (*arrestare*) _____ Alfonso.

c. nonostante (*essere*) _____ suo amico.

d. il cuoco Alfonso mette del veleno nel suo caffè.

cinque *Guarda la vignetta, lascia libera la fantasia e immagina cosa pensano il cardinale e il cuoco e completa i balloon.*

Riassunto episodio 6

Alem e Effe sono ancora nascosti nelle cucine vaticane quando, la mattina dopo, sentono le grida di gioia della folla che ha visto la fumata bianca. In quello stesso momento, in un'altra sala della cucina, il cuoco Alfonso mette qualcosa nel caffè del cardinale Stoppani, il nuovo Papa.

Zero entra e trova Effe e Alem: crede che siano loro i colpevoli e li fa arrestare: ma mentre Alem grida alle guardie che chi vuole uccidere il papa sono Zero e Gotor, Zero trova una bottiglietta. Alem gli dice che Alfonso l'ha appena usata per mettere qualcosa nel caffè del nuovo Papa e a questo punto Zero corre via: si sentono grida e spari e quando arrivano anche Alem e Effe trovano Gotor con una pistola in mano e Alfonso a terra: in verità Gotor è un agente dei servizi di sicurezza vaticani che insieme a Zero aveva il compito di proteggere il futuro Papa da possibili attentati. Grazie anche alla presenza di Effe e Alem il vero colpevole è stato scoperto e finalmente il nuovo Papa può affacciarsi al balcone per salutare la folla di fedeli.

Soluzioni

EPISODIO 1

1. 1/a; 2/b; 3/c; 4/c.

2. 1. *Effe lo aspetta*; 2. Due uomini nella macchina nera lo seguono; 3. Zero non lo saluta; 4. Zero gli consegna una busta; 5. Due uomini nella macchina nera gli sparano; 6. Alem ci vuole andare.

3. Mi, lo, Mi, si, Tu, ti; io, lei, Ti, me, Mi.

4. uscivo – ho incontrato – vedevo – ha salutato – ha dato – se ne è andato – è iniziata – conteneva – conoscevo – c'era – era – era – dicevano – sapevo – facevo – aveva dato – era scappato – sono uscito – mi sono accorto – stava – era.

EPISODIO 2

1. 1/c; 2/a; 3/a; 4/b.

2. Il cardinale Gotor è una figura misteriosa; il cardinale Stoppani ha combattuto per anni contro la mafia; Zero non vede Alem da molto tempo; Alem ha ricevuto una proposta di lavoro non rifiutabile; Michelangelo per quattro anni non ha permesso a nessuno di entrare nella Cappella Sistina.

3. del, nel, per, della, della, dell', per, della, nel, in, di, per, con.

4. a. cupola, b. statua, c. obelisco, d. piazza, e. colonnato, f. scalinata.

EPISODIO 3

1. 1/b; 2/a; 3/c; 4/a.

2. Alem deve andare a pranzo con Zero; Alem ha dei dubbi sul comportamento di Zero; Alfonso viene da Napoli; Effe fa la giornalista; Zero è convinto che il niovo Papa sarà il cardinale Stoppani; Zero sfugge alle domande di Alem.

3. 1-c, 2-a, 3-b.

4. è – abbia – importa – Sarà; ci sono stati – Sono – piacciano; potrebbe – sia – sono.

EPISODIO 4

1. 1/b; 2/b; 3/c; 4/b.

2. Effe ha ricevuto una notizia riservata riguardo al conclave; Alem non si fida di Zero; Il cardinale Gotor ha appuntamento con Zero; Zero entra in un passaggio segreto con il cardinale Gotor.

3. tanti – misteriosa – terribili – particolare – imprigionato – preziosissima – ricchissima – potentissima – famosa – fedele – morto

4. 1/c; 2/e; 3/a; 4/f; 5/d; 6/b.

5. Tutti vogliono che il cardinale Stoppani diventi Papa; Ho pensato che puoi aiutarmi a capire meglio; continua a non rispondermi

EPISODIO 5

1. 1/b; 2/b; 3/c; 4/c.

2. Effe prende la chiave nel vaso; Alem ha paura di essere scoperto; Il cardinale Gotor è un impostore; Zero dà un consiglio al cardinale Stoppani; Il cardinale Stoppani ha subito diversi attentati mafiosi.

3. 1/b; 2/c; 3/c; 4/a; 5/c; 6/a.

4. Effe ha chiesto ad Alem cosa aveva/avesse trovato; Alem ha detto a Effe che era la lista di tutti i cardinali partecipanti e che lì c'era c'è scritto che erano 101, non 102.

EPISODIO 6

1. 1/a; 2/c; 3/a; 4/c.

2. Alfonso mette del veleno nel caffè del nuovo Papa; Alem crede che l'assassino sia Zero; Zero fa arrestare Alem e Effe; Gotor ferisce Alfonso e lo arresta; Zero spiega tutto a Effe e Alem; Il cardinale Stoppani è salutato dalla folla di San Pietro.

3. criminali – protezione – custode – agente – sicurezza – azione – avvertire – salvo – annunciare.

4. 1. Dopo aver saputo che Stoppani era stato eletto Papa, il cuoco Alfonso mette del veleno nel suo caffè; 2. Zero vuole fare arrestare Alem nonostante sia suo amico; 3. Zero corre ad avvertire Renzi perché arresti Alfonso; 4. Alem e Effe avevano sempre creduto che Gotor fosse un assassino.

5. Risposta libera.